Lonely 🌐 planet

Offbeat

—— North America ——

100 AMAZING PLACES AWAY FROM THE TOURIST TRAIL

Intro

Our travel daydreams are rarely crowded. In your mind's eye, the Golden Gate Bridge is a marvel of engineering, not an obstacle course through cyclists and selfie sticks. You imagine Yellowstone's huffing geysers and rainbow-colored pools, not waiting for an hour to reach the park gate. But in reality, mass tourism has galloped into storied locations like these, accompanied by the four horsemen of noise, traffic, littering, and accidental photobombing.

Beyond its impact on the travel experience, overtourism does profound harm to the natural environment. Large numbers of people concentrated in a single place disturb wildlife, increase air and water pollution levels, and cause soil erosion from excessive footfall. Communities suffer too, especially when accommodation costs skyrocket and crowds overwhelm the rhythms of local life.

All travelers share the responsibility to ease this burden. To every one of us who has complained about a standstill traffic jam, there's an obvious rejoinder: 'You aren't stuck in traffic, you are traffic.' When we squeeze through a crowd to get a clear view of Niagara Falls, or walk double-speed in Yosemite to outpace a gaggle of hikers, we're not only hindered by overtourism, we're part of the phenomenon.

So where can a discerning traveler go to escape the crowds – and what does 'offbeat travel' even mean, in the digital age? After all, more than 98% of the inhabited world is now diligently charted on Google Maps. Meanwhile, language like "hidden gems" and "local secrets" has become a way to market destinations rather than protect them from the footprint of tourism.

That's why the impact of travel on our planet and people is at the forefront of this book. For more than 50 years, Lonely Planet has advocated for travel as a force for good: expanding travelers' minds, encouraging sustainable exploration and putting tourism dollars firmly in the hands of local businesses. It's in this spirit that we created *Offbeat North America*: a compendium of destinations across the 50 states, plus Canada, Mexico, and more, to inspire your travels.

Though the COVID-19 pandemic reset our habits, our hunger for travel has never been more voracious. Under lockdowns and travel restrictions, we explored our own neighborhoods with fresh eyes. We chose bikes, trains and cars over long-haul flights. But now, our wish lists are even longer than before, and we can finally satisfy our pent-up desires to explore.

There's a problem with snapping back to our old travel-hungry habits: the worldwide climate crisis is at boiling point, and tourism represents 8% of the world's carbon emissions. Although it took time for long-haul travel to bounce back after COVID, by late 2023 air traffic had reached more than 90% of pre-pandemic levels. So the challenge to travelers is this: how can we find the experiences we crave – sky-piercing mountains, golden sands or thought-provoking history – in a way that doesn't burden the landscapes and communities we visit?

This book is a springboard to answering that question. Inside these pages, you'll find alternatives to well-touristed locations that may inspire you to remix your North America bucket list. Instead of the Grand Canyon or Zion National Park, maybe Dead Horse Point (p. 103) could scratch your itch for red rock landscapes and boundless deserts. Perhaps your thirst for Napa Valley's wineries and rolling views could be unexpectedly quenched in Texas Hill Country (p. 141).

Some places will be familiar in name, though you might not have considered them as travel destinations; our features on Alabama (p. 229), Iowa (p. 175) and Missouri (p. 183) might change your mind. Meanwhile, a few places defy comparison with anywhere else in North America: for starters, Canada's 'Ukrainian Bloc' (p. 25), remarkably spiritual San Juan Chamula in Mexico (p. 309), and Assateague Island (p. 259) with its wild horses and shifting dunes. From unsung cities to the untamed outdoors, we hope they'll pique your curiosity for sustainable travels across this vast and varied continent.

Explore well,
Anita Isalska, Editor

Flint Hills, Kansas p. 179

St John's, Canada p. 45

South Dakota p. 159

Contents

100 AMAZING PLACES AWAY FROM THE TOURIST TRAIL

Dead Horse Point State Park, Utah p. 103

South Thomaston, Maine p. 295

This spread:
Kitimat Ranges, British Columbia

Canada

Haida Gwaii British Columbia

STORM-LASHED WILDERNESS AND FIRST NATIONS CULTURE ON REMOTE BC ISLANDS

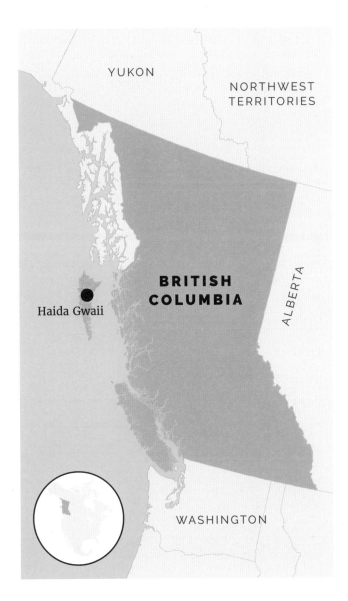

Wind-pummeled Haida Gwaii has an elemental, edge-of-the-world feel. Comprising a sword-shaped string of 450 islands, this remote archipelago is located 50 miles off the coast of British Columbia, near the Alaska border. Haida Gwaii is the ancestral home of the First Nations Haida people, who today make up half of the 4500-strong population and are paving a sustainable-tourism path with community-driven projects.

A deep regard for the natural environment is integral to Haida culture. Strict protection exists for Haida Gwaii's old-growth rainforests, craggy coastlines and diverse wildlife. As a result of the islands' geographic isolation, many species found here exist nowhere else on the planet. The entire southern third of the island chain is safeguarded by the wondrous 570 sq mile Gwaii Haanas National Park, where visitor numbers are kept deliberately low, ancient Haida sites await amid the coastal rainforest and kayaking is an off-grid joy for adventurous souls. Each year, only around 30,000 visitors make it across the Hecate Strait to Haida Gwaii – and it's worth every second of the journey.

GO IF YOU LIKE...
- ♥ *untouched wilderness*
- ♥ *First Nations culture*
- ♥ *wildlife*
- ♥ *community-led tourism*
- ♥ *Vancouver Island*
- ♥ *outdoor adventure*

Why go to Haida Gwaii?

Over 1.5 million birds, 20 types of whales and dolphins, rare sea otters, lazing sea lions and the world's largest black bear are just some of the archipelago's wildlife, which thrives in a pristine wilderness that's home to some of the planet's oldest red and yellow cedar trees.

The vast, unpopulated Gwaii Haanas National Park – a Unesco World Heritage Site – encompasses 138 islands, including Moresby. With hundreds of Haida sites located throughout the park, including a series of intricately carved oceanside memorial poles at SGang Gwaay, Gwaii Haanas is as much a testament to the region's Indigenous culture as an untrammeled natural wonderland. Haida caretakers keep watch at these sites during the spring-to-fall tourism season.

In recent years, Haida-owned accommodation, tour operators and other ventures have blossomed across the islands – all built around a key understanding of protecting both the natural environment and First Nations traditions.

GETTING THERE

BC Ferries link Skidegate Landing on Graham Island with Prince Rupert on the mainland three to six times a week (six to eight hours; bcferries.com). There are also year-round two-hour flights between Vancouver and Moresby Island's Sandspit airport, as well as northern Graham Island's smaller Masset airport.

WHEN TO GO

May – Oct

National park trips happen from spring to early fall. July and August are most popular, but May, June and September are quieter and equally enjoyable. May and June are ideal for spotting birds and whales; in September, black bears emerge to feast on salmon.

FIRST-TIME TIPS

Plan ahead for the national park; visitor numbers are capped and advance reservations are essential. The best way to visit is with a licensed operator such as Moresby Explorers (moresbyexplorers.com). Those visiting independently must join a Gwaii Haanas orientation.

....

There's limited public transport, so you'll need to rent a car. Alternatively, rent a bike.

....

Even during summer months, pack plenty of layers and warm clothing.

....

Stock up on farm-fresh produce, locally made treats and artisanal crafts at the islands' farmers markets; the popular Daajing Giids Farmers Market happens on Saturdays year-round.

Opposite page, **left:** Historic totem poles; **right:** sea lions on Anthony Island. **Above:** Exploring the mossy Pestua Trail

AMAZING CROWD-FREE EXPERIENCES

 Explore the Unesco-listed Gwaii Haanas National Park, National Marine Conservation Area Reserve and Haida Heritage Site, home to former Haida villages, centuries-old memorial poles, natural hot springs and sublime kayaking.

 Spot local wildlife — from bald eagles and sea lions to humpback whales, orcas and black bears — during migration season (March to October).

 Learn about Haida culture at the Haida Heritage Centre at Kay Llnagaay, near Skidegate, which introduces the islands' rich Indigenous traditions (haidaheritagecentre.com).

 Go hiking or kayaking in the ethereal Naikoon Provincial Park, where surf-whipped beaches, rock formations, dunes and peaceful pine-and-cedar forests await on northeast Graham Island.

 Discover traditional Haida crafts, such as woodcarving, weaving and jewelry making. Workshops and galleries like Tlell's Crystal Cabin welcome visitors (crystalcabingallery.com).

 Stay in an ocean- or river-view cabin at First Nations–owned Haida House on Graham Island's east coast, where Haida guides lead immersive excursions (haidatourism.ca).

Opposite: The North Pacific Cannery National Historic Site in Port Edward

Prince Rupert British Columbia

FIRST NATIONS CULTURE AND SUSTAINABLE CUISINE THRIVE AT THIS REMOTE PORT TOWN

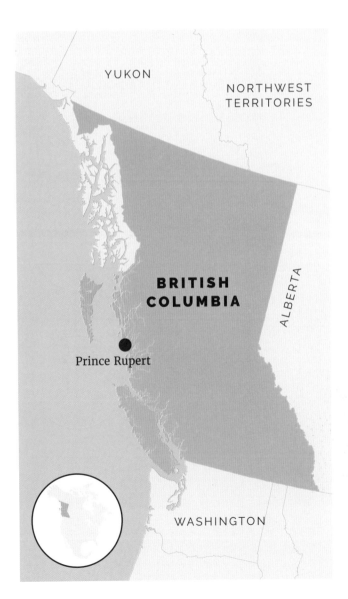

YUKON

NORTHWEST TERRITORIES

BRITISH COLUMBIA

ALBERTA

Prince Rupert

WASHINGTON

Tucked away in the far north of British Columbia, not far from the border with Alaska, Prince Rupert's watery locale could perhaps be described as Sydney Harbour without the crowds. Established in the early 20th century as the terminus of the Grand Trunk Pacific Railway, with hopes of rivaling Vancouver, Prince Rupert has developed instead into a relaxed secondary port city of 12,000 people, surrounded by some of the most impressive natural scenery Pacific Canada has to offer.

Located on Kaien Island, Prince Rupert has beautiful sea views from its waterfront and plenty more scenic attractions within an easy drive. Inland, the main highway and railway follow the course of the Skeena River, framed by misty mountain ranges and the occasional glacier. From the harbor itself, seaplanes host nature sightseeing tours to spot wildlife such as whales, eagles, salmon and bears. And the region is an ideal place for learning about the region's First Nations cultures, particularly at the Museum of Northern British Columbia with its exhibits of traditional crafts and regalia.

GO IF YOU LIKE...
- 💜 *Indigenous culture*
- 💜 *wildlife*
- 💜 *sustainable seafood*
- 💜 *mountainous scenery*
- 💜 *Alaska*

Why go to Prince Rupert?

It's rare nowadays to take in the majesty of nature without hordes of fellow travelers jostling your camera elbow. But Prince Rupert still allows space for contemplation of the sublime, especially beyond the city limits. Though it does receive cruise ships in summer, the passenger total is far lower than popular Alaskan destinations to the north, so it's easy to sidestep the masses when the ships are in.

Another reason to visit is the food. Prince Rupert's dining scene is on a roll, with dining venues placing an emphasis on cuisine connected to their community. Local sushi star Fukasaku has forged strong bonds with local fishermen using sustainable fishing methods, and Yaga Cafe Garden is a nonprofit cafe that helps fund First Nations language and culture revitalization schemes. There are plenty of other Asian flavors to taste in the city's restaurants, along with classic North American fare.

GETTING THERE

Flights connect Prince Rupert to Vancouver. An environmentally friendly option is to arrive by VIA Rail train from Vancouver, changing at Jasper. Prince Rupert is also a port on the Alaska ferry network, receiving vessels on the route from Bellingham, WA, to Alaskan ports Ketchikan, Sitka and Juneau. BC Ferries connects Prince Rupert to Port Hardy on Vancouver Island and to the islands of Haida Gwaii.

WHEN TO GO

May – Aug

The least rainy months to visit are from May to August, when days are also relatively warm. September is warm too, but distinctly wetter.

Below, left: Reflections in Cow Bay harbor; **right**: long-standing North Pacific Cannery. **Opposite:** The vertiginous rail route between Jasper and Prince Rupert

AMAZING CROWD-FREE EXPERIENCES

 Stand on the boardwalk of the North Pacific Cannery National Historic Site, admiring mist-shrouded hills and placid waters where an industrial facility once operated.

 Browse for a locally created bargain at the waterfront Lax Süülda Container Market, showcasing the output of regional artists and small businesses.

 Take a plane or boat to the Khutzeymateen Grizzly Bear Sanctuary, where you can safely view these imposing creatures as they roam freely in the wilderness.

 View Prince Rupert Harbour from the longhouse that hosts the Museum of Northern BC, before learning more about the local Ts'msyen people via its exhibits.

 Discover the history of the railway that helped create the city by visiting the Kwinitsa Railway Station Museum within a former station building.

 Ponder the fragility of life at the waterfront memorial housing the Kazu Maru, a fishing boat that drifted all the way from Japan after its owner was tragically lost at sea.

FIRST-TIME TIPS

Check the schedule for Prince Rupert's <u>cruise ship arrivals</u> *before your trip. You'll be able to avoid the water-borne crowds if you have some flexibility in your schedule and can arrive between cruises.*

....

If you're planning to fish while in the region, visit Fishery and Oceans Canada at dfo-mpo.gc.ca/ to get acquainted with the rules and to apply for a <u>fishing license.</u>

....

Familiarize yourself with the <u>Prince Rupert Travel Pledge</u> *(visitprincerupert.com), whose six points call on visitors to consider their impact on the local environment, people and culture.*

Ucluelet British Columbia

A NATURE-FOCUSED GETAWAY ON CANADA'S PACIFIC COAST

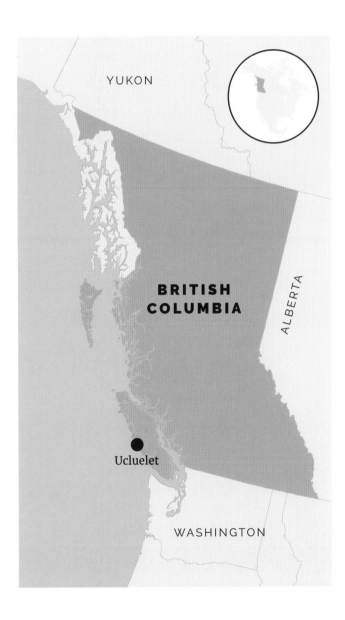

YUKON

BRITISH COLUMBIA

ALBERTA

Ucluelet

WASHINGTON

Many Canadians know Tofino, a hugely popular beach getaway on the far western shore of Vancouver Island – itself a hop, skip and a ferry ride from Vancouver city. But while the crowds continue to flock to this surfer's haven, a smaller number of in-the-know travelers are making their way twenty-five miles down the coast to tiny Ucluelet. Welcoming both day-trippers and overnighters, this workaday fishing village still retains the sleepy charms of yesteryear.

In Ucluelet, you might have to look a little harder for things to do, but you'll still find them, especially if you're planning a nature-focused getaway. There are rocky beaches to explore, quiet stretches of rainforest to hike in and peaceful roadways and paths to cycle. Ucluelet is home to Canada's first catch-and-release aquarium, where the sea creatures on view are returned to their nearby habitats every year. A growing number of locally focused places to eat have opened, too. And everywhere you look in Ucluelet is the wild Pacific, unfurling to a vast horizon.

GO IF YOU LIKE...
- *Tofino, BC*
- *Northern California*
- *rainforest hiking*
- *secluded coves*
- *local seafood*
- *winter storm watching*

Why go to Ucluelet?

In Ucluelet, start by getting outdoors. For hikers, the Wild Pacific Trail has several gentle to moderate routes with gorgeous views along the coast. Rent a sea kayak or reserve a kayaking tour from Ucluelet Harbour to explore the coast from the water, or book a whale-watching trip to see the majestic mammals swimming among the islands. Pacific Rim National Park Reserve, a protected area of sandy beaches and forest trails, sits between Ucluelet and Tofino and is easily accessible from either town.

Support local First Nations by booking an ocean-view cottage at Indigenous-owned Wya Point Resort. Ucluelet has a gourmet getaway, too. Pluvio Restaurant + Rooms, a four-room inn attached to a fine dining restaurant, is a fantastically creative spot for dinner, even if you're staying elsewhere. Sip vodka and gin made with wild yeast culture at Pacific Rim Distilling and toast your travels with a craft brew at Ucluelet Brewing.

GETTING THERE

Vancouver International Airport is the main gateway to western Canada. From Vancouver, you can reach Ucluelet by ferry and bus. BC Ferries travels from Horseshoe Bay north of Vancouver to Nanaimo's Departure Bay on Vancouver Island in 90 minutes. Tofino Bus picks up passengers at Departure Bay for the three-hour drive to Ucluelet.

WHEN TO GO

May – Oct

Ucluelet is a year-round destination; but for hiking, cycling and beach walking, the best times to visit are the drier spring through fall. July and August are busiest. Though very rainy, winter can be dramatic as Pacific storms roll in.

© MANUEL SULZER / GETTY IMAGES

FIRST-TIME TIPS

How do you pronounce Ucluelet? It's 'you-CLUE-let.'

Only one road, Hwy 4, crosses Vancouver Island to Ucluelet and Tofino. Before you set out, check DriveBC (drivebc.ca) for weather- or construction-related delays or road closures.

Take your time as you drive across the island. Stop to walk beneath the towering cedars and firs at Cathedral Grove, and enjoy the views from the twisting roadway over the mountains.

While it's easiest to explore Ucluelet and Vancouver Island's west coast with your own vehicle, the region is a good cycling destination. Several local companies rent bikes and e-bikes.

AMAZING CROWD-FREE EXPERIENCES

 Hike the Wild Pacific Trail, from a short loop past a lighthouse to a longer day-hike through the rainforest, with views over the ocean.

 Touch a crab or sea cucumber at Ucluelet Aquarium, which returns its specimens to their original habitats every year.

 Go whale watching to spot gray whales, humpbacks and orcas in the waters of Barkley Sound. Or opt for a bear-watching cruise.

 Take an e-bike tour along the coast, on the hunt for a local shipwreck.

 Have a beer in church – a smartly renovated former church, that is – now the home of Ucluelet Brewing Company.

 Book a locally focused dinner at Pluvio Restaurant, the town's top dining destination, where the inventive multicourse menus always feature seafood and produce from the region.

Clockwise from top: Vancouver Island's rocky shores; black bear stalking salmon; craft beers at Ucluelet Brewing Company; the Wild Pacific hiking trail

Ghost Towns of the Alberta Badlands Alberta

STAR IN YOUR VERY OWN WESTERN IN CENTURY-OLD SURROUNDS

BRITISH
COLUMBIA

ALBERTA

Ghost Towns of
the Alberta Badlands

SASKATCHEWAN

MONTANA

The well-preserved communities of Wayne, Rowley and Rosebud were once thriving mining and farming towns, and today their century-old clapboard buildings and Western surrounds look just like a film set. And indeed, the town of Rowley has served as the backdrop for so many movies – including Brad Pitt's box-office hit *Legends of the Fall* – that it's now called Rowleywood. Wayne, meanwhile, has a pub with bullet holes in its walls, though it was actually built to house coal miners in 1913. And Rosebud is a pretty prairie spot that was immortalized by Group of Seven painter AY Jackson in the summer of 1944.

GO IF YOU LIKE...
- 🤍 *ghost towns*
- 🤍 *performing arts*
- 🤍 *abandoned places*
- 🤍 *film sets*
- 🤍 *Canadian history*
- 🤍 *photography*

Following the opening of the Royal Tyrrell Museum in 1985, the town of Drumheller became a must-visit for dinosaur fanatics, and its colorful fossil beds and oddly shaped hoodoos continue to attract tourists in droves. But the vast majority of folks who make the trek here from Calgary or Edmonton often bypass one of the surrounding Badlands' most remarkable features: a cluster of three perfect ghost towns on the outskirts of Drumheller.

Why go to the ghost towns of the Alberta Badlands?

Rural Alberta isn't lacking in ghost towns, but most of them are little more than a derelict grain elevator or roadside monument. That's not the case with this trio, all of which are within a 25-mile radius of Drumheller.

First up is Rowley. Once home to five hundred souls, only a dozen people now call it home. Abandoned buildings sit on its outskirts – including a train station and three grain elevators – but the painstakingly restored main street is tailor-made for movie magic, with a funeral home, trading post and bank. Next is Wayne. During its coal-mining heyday, more than two thousand lived in the surrounding valley; now, only 25 people and a handful of buildings remain. Don't miss the Last Chance Saloon. Finally, there's Rosebud: the most well-known of the three, with 112 residents and the Rosebud School of the Arts, which stages productions year-round.

GETTING THERE

Drumheller is an 85-mile drive northeast of Calgary and a 175-mile drive south of Edmonton. Rosebud is 22 miles southwest of Drumheller, Rowley is 25 miles to the north and Wayne is 9 miles to the south. You'll need your own car; rentals are available in Edmonton and Calgary.

WHEN TO GO

May – Oct

The best part about ghost towns? There are no opening hours, and a dusting of morning frost can lend to the eerie vibes. However, the warmer months are when local events take place, including Rowley's legendary pizza nights.

Opposite: The arid badlands of Horseshoe Canyon. **Above**: Lively watering hole Sam's Saloon in Rowley

FIRST-TIME TIPS

You won't find any fuel, shops or ATMs. Pick up supplies in Drumheller, which caters to tourists.

Time your visit for Rowley's monthly pizza night, held the last Saturday of the month from May to August, with profits going towards the town's upkeep. Place your order at the local hall at 5pm and enjoy your pie while listening to local musicians.

There are several bed and breakfasts in Rosebud, including the 'Impossible Dream' windmill. Owned by a local actor, the historic three-story space is fully modernized and includes a trapdoor to a secret library.

AMAZING CROWD-FREE EXPERIENCES

 Drive across the 11 bridges to Wayne. Each of the single-lane bridges on Hwy 10X through the Rosebud River Valley is painted with its respective number.

 Take in a show at the Rosebud Theatre. Drumheller's outdoor Badlands Amphitheatre also hosts concerts and plays throughout the summer season.

 Spend the night in a ghost town. Dispersed camping is available in Rowley in designated areas near the grain elevators. Donations are appreciated.

 Go on a tour of Rowley. Local students offer free guided tours of building interiors between 10am and 6pm in July and August.

 Take a self-guided walking tour of Rosebud. Pick up your map in the Rosebud Centennial Museum, once the local laundry for miners.

 Hike through Horseshoe Canyon Trail. The striped canyon walls on this 3-mile walk reveal 70 million years of history, dating back to when dinosaurs roamed the earth.

'Ukrainian Bloc' Alberta

OUTRAGEOUS ROADSIDE ATTRACTIONS IN ALBERTA'S OFFBEAT CULTURAL MOSAIC

BRITISH COLUMBIA

ALBERTA

SASKATCHEWAN

● Ukranian Bloc

MONTANA

until roughly 1930 central Alberta was home to the largest colony of Ukrainian settlers in Canada. Today, this history lives on in the hamlets, ghost towns and communities that run along Hwys 16 and 28 east and northeast of Edmonton. A road trip through the region will reveal bakeries serving homemade cabbage rolls and the opportunity to see endemic wildlife in its native habitat, including bison.

Alberta's 'Ukrainian Bloc' is where Eastern European and Indigenous cultures collide, resulting in unique sights and culinary experiences – not to mention some truly outrageous roadside attractions.

D rive east of Edmonton and you'll soon be struck by the sheer number of big things. There's Vegreville's 2.5-ton pysanka (Ukrainian Easter egg), while in Mundare a giant ring of kovbasa (Ukrainian sausage) towers over the town. Further north in Glendon, a 26-foot-tall pierogi – complete with a fork speared through its center – welcomes visitors.

Small-town Canadians have a strange preoccupation with monster-sized objects. But why are so many Ukrainian-themed? As it turns out, from 1891

GO IF YOU LIKE...
- ♥ *giant attractions*
- ♥ *road trips*
- ♥ *wide-open spaces*
- ♥ *Eastern European food*
- ♥ *Canadian history*
- ♥ *stargazing*

Why go to Alberta's Ukrainian Bloc?

Alberta's Ukrainian Bloc is an easy day trip from Edmonton, with the Ukrainian Cultural Heritage Village – your first major stop – less than an hour away. It's best combined with a visit to Elk Island National Park (just across the road), which is home to free-roaming bison, elk, black bears and moose. But given its size (the exact boundaries are ill-defined, with the Bloc's reach extending roughly 150 miles northeast of Edmonton), this destination lends itself to a multiday road trip.

A lack of accommodation once posed a problem, but that's no longer the case thanks to Métis Crossing, just outside Smoky Lake. In 2022, the cultural center – which explores the history of the region's Métis people through interactive activities and workshops – opened a 40-room boutique lodge on the shores of the North Saskatchewan River. In 2023, it introduced sky-gazing domes with transparent ceilings, ideal for catching a glimpse of the northern lights.

FIRST-TIME TIPS

Bring a cooler. Smoky Lake's bakery stocks bags of frozen pierogies and borscht (beet soup). Similarly, Stawnichy in Mundare sells freezer packs of cabbage rolls, kielbasa sausage rings and perishke (cheese buns).

Time your visit to coincide with Smoky Lake's pumpkin festival, held in October. The event features pumpkin weigh-offs and a corn maze, but its highlight is when a massive pumpkin is dropped from a crane to smash a car below.

Map out the roadside attractions you'd like to stop at. Giant things range from Vilna's mushrooms to St Paul's UFO landing pad.

GETTING THERE

You can find communities with Ukrainian heritage running alongside Hwys 16 and 28 east and northeast of Edmonton all the way to Cold Lake. The Ukrainian Cultural Heritage Village is a 30-mile drive east of Edmonton, while Métis Crossing is a 75-mile drive northeast. There is no bus service, so you'll need to rent a car in Edmonton.

WHEN TO GO

May – Oct

Get behind the wheel before the snow hits the ground and winter road conditions set in. Some attractions, including the Ukrainian Cultural Heritage Village, are only open seasonally from late May until early September, so check opening hours in advance.

Opposite: White bison at Métis Crossing; **Above, left**: Aurora borealis dancing above Vilna; **right**: the Ukrainian Cultural Heritage Village

AMAZING CROWD-FREE EXPERIENCES

Follow the historic Victoria Trail. The oldest road in Alberta that's still in regular use, this 36-mile route follows the North Saskatchewan River to Victoria Settlement, a historic fur-trading post.

Watch the northern lights dance. Positioned under the auroral oval and free of light pollution, northeastern Alberta is one of the best places to see the aurora borealis, particularly in autumn.

Go where the buffalo roam. Elk Island National Park is home to both plains and wood bison, while Métis Crossing's Wildlife Park has rare white bison.

Step back in time at the Ukrainian Cultural Heritage Village. A re-creation of Alberta's historic Ukrainian settlements, with interpreters in period costume.

Paddle into the past on the North Saskatchewan River. Travel in a historic Voyageur canoe from Victoria Settlement to Métis Crossing.

Bring your camera to capture images of silver-domed Ukrainian churches set against a backdrop of brilliant yellow canola fields.

Grasslands National Park Saskatchewan

FAR-FLUNG WILDLIFE HAVEN WHERE BISON AND ARCHAEOLOGISTS ROAM

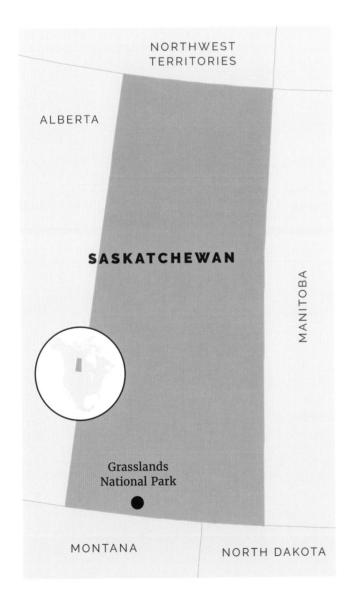

NORTHWEST TERRITORIES

ALBERTA

SASKATCHEWAN

MANITOBA

Grasslands National Park

MONTANA

NORTH DAKOTA

Grassland ecosystems are the unsung heroes of the climate crisis, with the ability to sequester and store billions of tons of carbon. But they're also becoming increasingly rare. Considered one of the world's most endangered ecosystems, southern Saskatchewan's Grasslands National Park is one of the only places to see them.

A place of rugged coulees, badlands and vast stretches of mixed-grass prairies, Grasslands is also where some of Canada's most unique species thrive. Plains bison wander freely through the fields, rare burrowing owls live in abandoned gopher holes and Canada's only remaining black-tailed prairie dogs live in large colonies. Add in quicksand, one of Canada's richest dinosaur fossils beds and thousands of archaeological sites, and pretty soon you'll feel like Indiana Jones.

The explorer vibes will only be reinforced by the sensation that you have the park all to yourself. Despite its otherworldly beauty, Grasslands remains one of the country's least-visited national parks. While heavy hitters like Jasper and Banff attract millions every year, only about 17,500 people visit Grasslands annually.

GO IF YOU LIKE…
- ♥ *wildlife*
- ♥ *stargazing*
- ♥ *hiking*
- ♥ *archaeology*

Why go to Grasslands National Park?

It's not uncommon to drive through Grasslands National Park – even in the peak of summer – without seeing anyone else. Instead, you'll be surrounded by the sound of prairie dogs chirping, coyotes howling in the coulees below and bison bellowing across the prairies.

The park is split into two blocks, with most visitors gravitating towards the West Block, which is serviced by the gateway community Val Marie. A tiny hamlet with a thriving arts scene, it offers a few basic amenities, including the park's visitor center, a restaurant, a small grocery store and some accommodation. The West Block also has more established hiking trails and more wildlife, including its large herd of plains bison.

However, the East Block is equally worth visiting. A stunning landscape of badlands that's frequented by paleontologists for its density of fossils, it's a must-see for photographers, with the relatively new 7-mile Badlands Parkway carrying visitors deep into the wild prairie expanse.

GETTING THERE

Grasslands' two blocks are found along the Saskatchewan–Montana border, southwest of Regina. From Regina to Val Marie – the West Block's gateway – it's 220 miles. To the East Block, it's 175 miles. There is no bus service, so you'll need to drive. Car rental is available in Regina.

WHEN TO GO

May – Oct

Visit in May or June to see abundant wildflowers and migrating wildlife, or in the late summer or fall for more moderate temperatures. Although the park is open year-round, there are no services in winter.

AMAZING CROWD-FREE EXPERIENCES

 Pitch a tent where no one has before. Backcountry camping is permitted throughout Grasslands National Park within designated zones.

 Soak in the silence. According to acoustic ecologist Gordon Hempton, Grasslands National Park is one of the quietest places on earth.

 Grasslands is home to one of Canada's largest and darkest Dark Sky Preserves. On select summer weekends, astronomers lead guided tours of the night sky.

 Watch for signs of the past. Evidence of the park's 10,000 years of human habitation include 20,000 tipi rings found throughout the park and 80-million-year-old fossils.

 Choose your own adventure. You can walk anywhere in the park (no trail necessary) or choose from one of the established paths ranging from 0.5 to 10 miles in length.

 Spend an afternoon exploring the West Block's ecotour scenic drive. Marked by interpretative panels, the 12.4-mile route includes stops at prairie dog colonies, archaeological sites and historic homesteads.

Opposite, left: Backcountry camping in the badlands; **right**: magical light and 70 Mile Butte in the distance. **Below**: Black-tailed prairie dogs keeping watch

Manitoulin Island Ontario

EXPLORE INDIGENOUS CULTURES ON THE WORLD'S LARGEST FRESHWATER ISLAND

an excellent place to learn about Indigenous cultures. The largest, Wiikwemkoong First Nation, has a well-developed cultural tourism program, which welcomes visitors interested in their heritage and society.

By road from Toronto, Ontario's largest city, it's 340 miles to Manitoulin, crossing the historic Swing Bridge that leads to Little Current, the island's main town. You can cut your driving time slightly by catching the ferry from the Bruce Peninsula, northwest of Toronto. No matter how you get to this quiet Canadian island, though, your trip can include both enlightening cultural experiences and relaxing time outdoors.

Manitoulin Island is the biggest freshwater island in the world. Reaching this large, and largely rural, northern Ontario isle, where country roadways wind between forests and fields, takes some effort. But for those who savor hiking on uncrowded trails, poking around in community museums and swimming in crisp cool lakes, it's worth the journey.

Part of Canada's Lake Huron, Manitoulin encompasses the traditional territories and present-day communities of six First Nations, making it

GO IF YOU LIKE…
- *Indigenous cultures*
- *lake beaches*
- *fish and chips*
- *rural roadways*
- *small-town life*
- *temperate islands*

Why go to Manitoulin Island?

If you come to Manitoulin by ferry, you'll arrive on the south shore, which is a short drive from the curving sands of Providence Bay, the island's best beach. With light-filled loft-style apartments above a hip cafe and gallery, the island's coolest accommodation, Mutchmor Lofts, is a short walk from the beach.

Driving onto the island brings you to Little Current, the largest town, where guest rooms at First Nations–owned Manitoulin Hotel and Conference Centre incorporate Indigenous designs. Southwest of Little Current, at the Ojibwe Cultural Foundation on the M'Chigeeng First Nation, you can learn about Anishinaabe culture and art. Nearby, Lillian's Crafts and Museum exhibits porcupine quillwork, a traditional craft, and sells artwork, jewelry and other items by Indigenous creators.

The unceded territory of the Wiikwemkoong First Nation occupies Manitoulin's east end, where you can choose from several Indigenous cultural experiences, including guided hikes, history tours and cooking workshops.

GETTING THERE

The easiest way to reach Manitoulin Island from Toronto Pearson International Airport is by car and ferry. Drive northwest from Toronto to the Bruce Peninsula, where the MS *Chi-Cheemaun* ferry transports passengers and vehicles between Tobermory and Manitoulin Island. Operated by the Owen Sound Transportation Company, the ferry runs mid-May to mid-October; the crossing takes two hours.

WHEN TO GO

Jun – Sep

Many Manitoulin businesses operate only from June through September. For a quiet getaway, consider May or October, but check what's open. The *Chi-Cheemaun* ferry operates from late spring into fall; at other times you'll need to drive from the north.

AMAZING CROWD-FREE EXPERIENCES

 Learn about Indigenous culture when you join a guide from the Wiikwemkoong Nation to walk through local history, forage for edible plants or cook venison or trout over an open fire.

 Hike the Cup and Saucer Trail that climbs to a lookout with views across the island.

 Go to a powwow, an Indigenous cultural celebration with traditional dances, drumming and food. While most of Manitoulin's First Nations host powwows, Wiikwemkoong Annual Cultural Festival Powwow (August) is the island's largest.

 Take an archaeological tour, exploring the Sheguiandah Archeological Site, where evidence of human life dates back more than 10,000 years.

 Watch a performance by the Debajehmujig Theatre Group, an Indigenous company, that normally stages their shows during the summer months.

 Chow down on your favorite fish and chips, made from local whitefish. Lake Huron Fish and Chips in Providence Bay fries up a top contender.

Above: Bridal Veil Falls, flowing from Lake Kagawong

FIRST-TIME TIPS

Most Manitoulin communities have somewhere to eat or buy groceries, although many keep <u>limited hours</u>, especially outside the peak summer months of July and August. Don't assume you can run into the market or sit down to dinner after 8pm.

⋯⋯⋯⋯⋯⋯⋯⋯⋯⋯⋯⋯⋯⋯⋯⋯⋯⋯

Allow more time to get around the island than distances might indicate. <u>Manitoulin's roads are slow</u> and meandering.

⋯⋯⋯⋯⋯⋯⋯⋯⋯⋯⋯⋯⋯⋯⋯⋯⋯⋯

Attending a powwow? These Indigenous events are alcohol- and drug-free, so please <u>respect those rules</u>. Photography and video are normally allowed, except during certain ceremonies or dances; the powwow host will let spectators know when to put down your camera.

Algonquin Provincial Park Ontario

A LAKE-LACED WONDERLAND CAPTURES ONTARIO'S WILD NATURAL BEAUTY

ONTARIO

QUEBEC

Algonquin Provincial
Park

MINNESOTA

WISCONSIN

MICHIGAN

IOWA

The region's original inhabitants, the Indigenous Algonquin people, lived here for centuries before Europeans arrived in the 1800s and a local logging industry was born. Today, Algonquin encompasses almost 2400 lakes, 1200 miles of canoeing routes and 85 miles of hiking trails and welcomes around 1 million visitors each year. For contrast, Alberta's similarly sized Banff National Park receives around 3.7 million annual visitors.

When you paddle across an inky lake reflecting a marshmallow-pink sunset, hike through rust-colored fall maples to a viewpoint or glimpse a moose hidden in the forest canopy, Algonquin feels like leaving the world behind.

Canada's western provinces might hog the spotlight when it comes to vast, untouched natural places, but Ontario has its own spectacular wilderness. Established in 1893, Algonquin is the country's oldest provincial park and holds a special place in the heart of Canadians. Sprawling across 2900 sq miles, this massive expanse of forest fringes sparkling cobalt lakes where moose, loons, black bears, foxes, otters, wolves and other wildlife roam.

GO IF YOU LIKE...
- *wild landscapes*
- *canoeing*
- *Banff and Jasper*
- *emblematic Canadian wildlife*
- *camping*
- *fall colors*

Why go to Algonquin Provincial Park?

Algonquin's lake-dotted landscapes famously inspired the Canadian artist Tom Thomson and the Group of Seven painters, whose legacy lives on in a still-thriving local art scene. Get a taste at the Algonquin Art Centre (algonquinartcentre.com). Hike out to an escarpment overlooking white-pine forests, paddle across a lake to a blissfully isolated campsite, sit on the shore to drink in a pastel-hued sunrise – it's all part of the go-slow Algonquin experience.

The meandering Hwy 60 traverses the park's southernmost end, home to a handful of campsites; but this is just a tiny slice of a rolling, densely forested haven where escaping into nature is easy. Fresh investment is now being channeled into creating and restoring yurts and cabins and upgrading hiking trails. Visit midweek, in spring, fall or even winter, or head off on a multiday backcountry canoe trip, and you'll often have the entire place to yourself.

GETTING THERE

Algonquin Provincial Park is about three hours' drive north of Toronto; the best way to get here is with your own wheels. There are also a few summer buses from Toronto with Parkbus (three to four hours; parkbus. ca). Algonquin Visitors Centre is at Km 43 on Hwy 60 and has an excellent museum; two more information offices await near the East and West Gates.

WHEN TO GO

May, Jun, Sep, Oct

Spring is great for moose-spotting and canoe trips (bring protection against blackflies from mid-May). Fall colors burst into action from September on, typically peaking at the month's end. This is also an ideal time for hiking and canoeing – without bugs!

FIRST-TIME TIPS

Almost all accommodation within the park is in Ontario Parks' 11 car-accessible campgrounds (ontarioparks.com). There are also remote backcountry campsites reached only by hiking, canoeing or skiing. Book well ahead, especially for summer.

For the main campgrounds, secluded sites near a lakefront or with direct water access are particularly tempting.

Stay as many nights as possible to be fully immersed in nature; skip long weekends in summer; and check up-to-date regulations before heading over (algonquinpark.on.ca).

Three privately operated lodges are located within the park, including rustic-charm Killarney Lodge on Lake of Two Rivers (killarneylodge.com).

AMAZING CROWD-FREE EXPERIENCES

 Soak up Algonquin's serenity on a multinight backcountry canoe trip with the Portage Outpost. Or hire a canoe for a day's exploring (algonquinoutfitters.com).

 Keep an eye out for wildlife. Dawn and dusk (especially in May and June) are the best times to spot moose, often lurking in marshy areas and along Hwy 60.

 Start or end the day with a swim in a glinting lake, often with just the chirping birds for company.

 See Algonquin in winter. From November to March, the park transforms into a snow-covered paradise.

 Tackle a thrilling hike such as the 6.5-mile Centennial Ridges Trail (dazzling forest views) or the 4.8-mile Track and Tower Trail (taking in an abandoned railway).

 Head out on two wheels, perhaps tackling the challenging summer-only Minnesing Trail (up to 20 miles).

Clockwise from top left: Cozy Killarney Lodge; bull moose taking a dip; exploring the park on a canoe made for two

Gaspé Peninsula Quebec

DISCOVER THE CLIFFS AND BEACHES OF THIS REMOTE FRANCOPHONE REGION

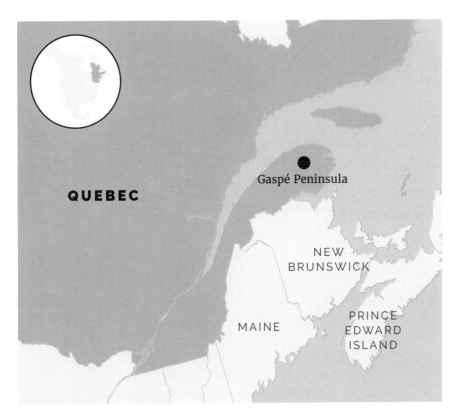

Learn about the evolution of fish at a unique regional park and tour museums of Acadian heritage and maritime disasters. While none of the communities around La Gaspésie are especially large, tourism is centered around the town of Gaspé at the peninsula's tip, closest to Parc national de Forillon. Nearby Percé is known both for a landmark rock and for North America's largest migratory bird sanctuary. And everywhere you go on the Gaspé, you can dig into freshly caught seafood: shrimp, clams and especially lobster.

GO IF YOU LIKE...
- coastal Maine
- Nova Scotia
- ocean bird life
- national parks
- Québécois culture
- fresh seafood

Québec's Gaspé Peninsula juts into the Gulf of St Lawrence, where its waterfront highway hugs the cliffs above the sea. Road-tripping through this far-flung francophone region, northeast of Québec City, you can stop to spot unusual seabirds, go whale watching or wander along the water in a secluded national park. There are offshore islands to explore, maritime mountains to hike and sandy beaches all around, as the landscape varies from forested peaks to the sea as far as the eye can see.

Why go to Gaspé Peninsula?

Many Gaspé highlights are outdoors, including the gorgeous Parc national de Forillon at the peninsula's Land's End, where you can hike, camp, kayak, paddleboard and more. A boat trip from Percé brings you to Île Bonaventure, where the large seabird known as the gannet makes its home. Take a virtual voyage at Musée de la Gaspésie, where a recently launched virtual reality exhibit lets you live like a 1960s fisherman. Check out the International Garden Festival at historic Reford Gardens with innovative exhibitions, or visit Musée Acadien du Québec in Bonaventure for stories of Québec's Acadians, who settled this region in the 1700s.

For a new adventure, go canyoneering in the Chic Choc mountains with Eskamer Aventure. The Gaspé has several recently opened accommodations, too, whether you stay above the sea in the Scandinavian-style Nautika Chalets, book a forest getaway at stylish [ÈST] Éco-cabines or go glamping in the yurts at Domaine Tourelle-sur-Mer.

GETTING THERE

Québec City is the nearest gateway to the Gaspé Peninsula; fly into Jean Lesage International Airport (YQB) or take the Via Rail train. Ferries cross to the Gaspé town of Matane from the north shore of the St Lawrence. While the easiest way to explore the peninsula is with your own vehicle, Orléans Express buses connect Montréal and Québec City with several Gaspé communities.

WHEN TO GO

May – early Oct

May and June are lobster season in the Gaspé and seafood is at its freshest. While most visitors arrive in the peak summer months of July and August, autumn, from September into early October, has gorgeous fall foliage.

FIRST-TIME TIPS

When you're road-tripping around the Gaspé, loop the peninsula in a counter-clockwise direction. You'll keep the water on your right, where it's easier to take in the views and stop for photos.

While most Gaspé visitors head for the water, it's worth traveling inland, too. Parc national de la Gaspésie lures hikers with its mountain summits, which are among the highest in Québec.

If you speak any French, residents will appreciate your bonjours and mercis.

Many Gaspé residents are of Acadian heritage, and you'll spot the Acadian red, white and blue flag with a gold star flying above many homes.

Opposite, left: Driving coastal Route 132; **right**: the Grand Gathering sculptures in Sainte-Flavie. **Above:** An offshore refuge for white gannets

AMAZING CROWD-FREE EXPERIENCES

Go gaga over gannets when you cruise to Parc national de l'Île-Bonaventure-et-du-Rocher-Percé, an offshore refuge for this photogenic seabird.

Hike to Land's End, paddleboard in Gaspé Bay or scout for seals by sea kayak in Parc national de Forillon at the peninsula's tip.

Explore ancient fish fossils at Parc national de Miguasha, the world's premier site illustrating the Devonian period more than 350 million years ago.

Spot blue whales, humpbacks and other marine mammals on a whale-watching adventure in the Gulf of St Lawrence.

Overnight with the wolves when you book a cabin at Bioparc Gaspésie and explore this nature park after dark.

Gape at sculptures marching out of the St Lawrence, an unusual art installation called *Le Grand Rassemblement* (The Great Gathering) that local artist Marcel Gagnon created in the riverside village of Ste Flavie.

St John's Newfoundland

THE LAST OF THE MARITIMES, HALFWAY TO GREENLAND

NEWFOUNDLAND

QUEBEC

ONTARIO

St John's

At North America's eastern edge, you can almost imagine looking out from Cape Spear Lighthouse and catching a glimpse of Ireland. When you hear the locals chatting it up in the pubs on George Street, the impressions of Old Erin are magnified – 26 local dialects are traced back to Irish immigrants, and their music endures in the lively nightlife and maritime songs. You can go no further east in North America than St John's, yet you'll feel right in the middle of something special.

Just offshore are some of the largest seabird colonies in the world: clownlike puffins sporting tricolored bills, magnificent gannets piercing the sapphire seas like gold-and-white arrows. On solid ground,

massive caribou wander the lichen-dappled boulders of this southernmost tundra, its sawn-off shrubbery a testament to both the whipping winds and nature's resilience. You're likely to see whales off Mistaken Point Ecological Preserve, and in the evenings tuck into some of the heartiest fish meals you've ever tasted, washed down with a pint or two.

GO IF YOU LIKE…
- 💜 *folk music*
- 💜 *windswept lighthouses*
- 💜 *puffins*
- 💜 *the great outdoors*
- 💜 *fish and chips*

Why go to St John's?

Even if you've been to Canada's urban centers, nothing can prepare you for the charm and untamed edge that is St John's. Canada only 'joined' Newfoundland in 1949, and the sense of independence from the mainland is palpable — a culture apart, alive in every lilting accent.

Local B&Bs along the developing East Coast Trail get you up close and personal with the locals, generations of fisherfolk with ocean water coursing their veins. Well-appointed restaurants go beyond fishy fare and include vegan, Thai, Japanese and Italian options. Or go local with a 'jiggs dinner' – root veggies and a side of salt (corned) beef.

Scale Signal Hill, where Guglielmo Marconi received the first transatlantic radio waves, and view the fields where aviators like John Alcock and Arthur Brown (who crossed the sea eight years before Lindbergh) and Amelia Earhart first cast their eyes on the glory and pain of traversing the mighty Atlantic by plane.

GETTING THERE

St John's is, well, out there. It's a three-hour plane ride from Montreal or Toronto. Ferry service will get you from the mainland – either Québec or Nova Scotia – to Newfoundland (Port aux Basques, seven hours; Argentia, 16 hours). Rent a car once you arrive.

WHEN TO GO

Jun – Sep

Summer has the best weather for hiking, wildlife-watching and outdoor festivals. August's Royal St John's Regatta on Quidi Vidi Lake is America's longest-running sporting event; downtown St John's becomes a convivial pedestrian mall in July and August.

FIRST-TIME TIPS

Locals say you can experience all four seasons in a St John's day. It's true, so come prepared.

St John's is a charming city, but you'd be cheating yourself if you didn't get out to Witless Bay to see the whales, puffins, and other amazing critters.

It's a mite easier to mingle in the taverns on weeknights and get your dose of music and conversation in a less-hectic setup.

Open mics and live music abounds, including the Newfoundland and Labrador Folk Music Society sessions at the renowned Ship Pub.

AMAZING CROWD-FREE EXPERIENCES

 Revel in the sea breezes and serenity of the East Coast Trail. This network of 25 different trails winds for 209 miles around the Avalon Peninsula.

 Find Mile 0 of the Trans Canada Trail, marked at Cape Spear, the continent's easternmost point.

 Visit Mistaken Point, named for the many ships wrecked off its coast. It's also rich in Precambrian fossils.

 Hike to Quidi Vidi for an iceberg ale while looking down on eagles' nests and, maybe, a real iceberg.

 Find a peaceful moment in an old stone church. Anglicans and Catholics named their temples of worship for the city's patron saint.

 Charter a more intimate boat tour from Quidi Vidi harbor and immerse yourself in the life of local fisherfolk.

Clockwise from top: Hiking the windswept East Coast Trail; the lighthouse at at Cape Spear Historic Site; a rainbow-beaked resident puffin

This spread: Kennecott Mines, Alaska

West
USA

Dalton Highway Alaska

ONE OF AMERICA'S MOST CHALLENGING ROADS

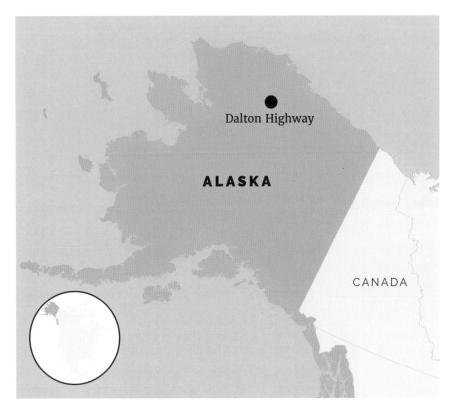

Operating primarily as a haul road for the oil industry, the Dalton is a rough, potholed and dusty transection of Arctic Alaska wilderness. But those who choose to explore the traditional lands of the Athabascan and Inupiat peoples will find history, culture, recreation and a tenacity for life that is unequaled in other destinations around the state.

Few visitors to Alaska venture this far north due to a lack of both facilities and time. To drive the entire distance requires patience. You'll need to be comfortable averaging only 30 to 50 mph on rough terrain, all the while yielding to 18-wheeled semitrucks roaring across the gravel on their way to Deadhorse.

Alaska's 498-mile Dalton Highway is no ordinary road trip. Beginning 80 miles north of Fairbanks, this mostly gravel highway winds through boreal forest, untamed rivers, rugged tundra and towering mountain passes. Built to facilitate natural resource extraction and yet traveling through some of the world's most pristine landscapes, the Dalton Highway reflects the often difficult tug between progress and sacred spaces.

GO IF YOU LIKE...
- *wilderness road trips*
- *national parks*
- *camping and hiking*
- *Alaska*
- *remote destinations*
- *a challenge*

51

Why travel the Dalton Highway?

Perhaps no other place in Alaska provides the adventure-seeking visitor with the experience of being completely alone, on a highway, in the United States. In a time where many national parks have become so crowded that they require reservations to enter, traveling the Dalton Highway feels liberating, both physically and emotionally. Where else can one see both the Trans-Alaska Pipeline and a grizzly bear scrabbling for small game at its base, or float down the Koyukuk River past log cabins that look like they're straight out of a Jack London novel?

For all its challenges, the Dalton Highway is a self-sufficient camper's dream destination. With several campsite options available between Fairbanks and the Arctic Circle's Coldfoot, most people won't ever see more than a handful of other travelers. Take the time to drive slowly, savor the views and ponder the inherent contradictions of the highway.

GETTING THERE

Many people fly in for a day, take some photos and then fly out. But if you're driving, the right type of vehicle is a must. Only a handful of rental agencies permit travel on the Dalton; check with resources in Fairbanks for a list. Several tour companies out of Fairbanks also offer group tours, with overnight stays in Coldfoot available.

WHEN TO GO

late Jun – mid-Aug

While the highway is open all year, most visitors drive this road during the summer months when lingering daylight affords the safest travel.

Opposite, top: Sawtooth Sukakpak Mountain; **bottom**: Northern lights over Brooks Mountains

AMAZING CROWD-FREE EXPERIENCES

 Stop at the Arctic Interagency Visitor Center in Coldfoot for information, weather conditions and facts about the local flora and fauna.

 Tour the oil patch facilities and dip your toes into the Arctic Ocean. Make reservations through Deadhorse Camp at least 24 hours in advance.

 Seek views of the northern lights between late August and early April. Guided tours make the most sense as winter is decidedly more hazardous. Northern Alaska Tour Company offers winter trips up the Dalton Highway

 Take a photo at the Arctic Circle sign at a campground near mile 115.6.

 Raft the Koyukuk River with a Coldfoot Camp guide, learning about the area's geography, flora and fauna.

 Watch for birds. More than two hundred species inhabit the Dalton Highway corridor, including willow ptarmigan (Alaska's state bird), Smith's longspur and various raptors. Spot blue whales, humpbacks and other marine mammals on a whale-watching adventure in the Gulf of St Lawrence.

FIRST-TIME TIPS

Always travel with extra food, water, clothing and a first-aid kit. There are no medical services, stores or flush toilets along the Dalton Highway.

....

Beware of steep road grades, mud and potholes. There are no road services available should your vehicle break down. Yield to industry vehicles: pull over and let them pass.

....

Take your time. Allow two or more days to reach Coldfoot and then Deadhorse/Prudhoe Bay, which will give you more time to appreciate the raw wilderness.

....

Stop and stretch your legs at Yukon Camp (mile 56) and Finger Rock (mile 96).

McCarthy & Kennecott Alaska

AN UNSPOILED SLICE OF THE LAST FRONTIER IN THE COUNTRY'S LARGEST NATIONAL PARK

Surrounded by icy peaks (nine of the country's 16 highest mountain ranges are found in Wrangell-St Elias), McCarthy and Kennecott are kissing-cousin remnants of a once-thriving copper industry that built an entire mill town and supply center more than one hundred miles from the nearest city in the early 20th century. Although the mine closed in 1938, the National Park Service has refurbished the once-decrepit Kennecott mill site as a national historic landmark, while McCarthy has grown as an off-the-grid, funky place to access adventure activities like white-water rafting, ice climbing and hiking.

GO IF YOU LIKE...
- ♥ *hiking and climbing*
- ♥ *rafting*
- ♥ *self-sufficient travel*
- ♥ *national parks*
- ♥ *Alaska history*
- ♥ *remote road trips*

F ar from Alaska's bustling cruise ship docks and crowded attractions is Wrangell-St Elias National Park, featuring the rugged wilderness – and people – of Alaska lore. This sprawling 20,000 sq mile chunk of Alaska's southeast mainland provides excellent insight into the state's lengthy relationship with mining, subsistence lifestyles and adrenaline-fueled adventure. Snuggled within the park at its south end is a 60-mile gravel road that leads visitors to the tiny communities of McCarthy and Kennecott.

Why go to McCarthy and Kennecott?

Most visitors to Alaska merely skim the surface of the state's landscapes, culture and colorful people who give 'independent' a new meaning. Getting to rural communities like Kennecott and McCarthy requires tenacity, but it's easy to get swept up in the adventurous spirit possessed by early homesteaders and miners.

There are pristine alpine landscapes and a decided lack of tour buses and one-and-done visitors checking off a bucket list of sights. Only about 65,000 people visit Wrangell–St Elias National Park annually, compared to the nearly 300,000 who flock to Denali each year.

With no paved roads or shopping centers, and few private vehicles, McCarthy and Kennecott make for an unhurried experience. From following local trails traveled by generations of humans and wildlife, to perusing newspapers, work logs and school essays from the mining days, the McCarthy–Kennecott experience is a gift, and one to treat reverently.

GETTING THERE

Reaching McCarthy-Kennecott takes careful planning and a good deal of time. Most visitors arrive via regular flights from the town of Chitina, and there are also select flights from Anchorage via mail plane; book early. To truly experience Alaska's vast distances, however, driving is best. From Anchorage, figure on seven to eight hours.

WHEN TO GO

Jul & Aug

The National Park Service closes just after Labor Day in early September and doesn't open again until late May at the earliest. Visitors have a short window to explore; July and August are best.

FIRST-TIME TIPS

Driving? Check with rental companies ahead of time. Many will not allow vehicles to travel the Edgerton Highway because of the gravel surface and unpredictable conditions.

Plan to walk. A lot. Vehicles not registered to residents are prohibited in McCarthy-Kennecott. It's an easy walk from the end of the highway to town, and a regular shuttle travels the five miles between the two communities throughout the day.

Pack for mountain weather. Rain, snow and bright sunshine can occur at any time. Bring warm, waterproof layers, sunscreen, drinking water, appropriate footwear and a comfortable backpack.

AMAZING CROWD-FREE EXPERIENCES

 Hop in a raft or kayak and float the river from McCarthy.

 Relax at Kennicott Glacier Lodge. Spelled with an 'i' as an homage to the nearby glacier, the lodge is a historical marvel stuffed with artifacts. It's the only lodging available at the mill site.

 Walk on ice at Root Glacier. Explore the icy flanks of a glacier on a gentle hike or kick your crampons into the ice on a guided climb.

 Hike to abandoned mines. The scenery alone makes the heart-pumping switchbacks worth it.

 Take a road trip from Anchorage. It's a seven- to eight-hour journey through muskeg and boreal forest, along the fringes of Wrangell-St Elias via the Edgerton Highway (McCarthy Road).

 Take a walking tour of the Kennecott Mill Site and town. Both guided and self-guided tours are available.

Clockwise from top left: Gleaming copper nuggets; Kennecott mill town and mines; exploring ice caves at Root Glacier

Opposite: Snow-capped cliffs at Kings Bay, south of Whittier

Whittier Alaska

ISOLATED FISHING VILLAGE BUILT AND ABANDONED BY THE US ARMY

ALASKA

CANADA

Whittier

base for deployed American soldiers – a heavily fortified Cold War hideout just 775 miles from Russia. After the Army jumped ship in the 1960s, Whittier called on tourism (kayaking, fishing and glacier-viewing) to ward off ghost-town status. Today, the town's military installations make up the Whittier Army Port Historical District; all three hundred or so residents live in one of two buildings, the biggest of which was the Army's largest construction since the Pentagon when it was erected in 1956.

GO IF YOU LIKE...
- *military history*
- *alpine landscapes*
- *boat journeys*
- *the Cold War*
- *abandoned buildings*
- *wildlife*

Whittier, a small fishing harbor in Prince William Sound, is located 60 miles southwest of Anchorage, Alaska's largest city. Although it's not far as the crow flies, Whitter can only be accessed via ferry or North America's longest highway tunnel. Driving through the 2.5-mile one-lane Anton Anderson Memorial Tunnel, which is shared by cars and trains alike, takes around 12 minutes; the journey, however, feels like a decades-long leap into America's Cold War past. This bizarre outpost was constructed by the US Army in 1941 as a military intake

Why go to Whittier?

Taking a boat or sea-kayaking trip on Prince William Sound – surrounded by sea otters, humpback whales, bald eagles and imposing glaciers – is a fantastic way to spend an Alaskan day. However, day-trippers and cruise ship passengers usually miss Whittier's beguiling story on land. A quirky, architectural time capsule showcasing both military might and US Army excess, Whittier's back streets combine the thrill of abandoned town exploration with the seeming transgression of wandering a military installation without authorization.

Today, ex-Army apparatuses, such as the former vehicle service center and the troop gymnasium, have been reborn as seafood processing plants and boat sheds, respectively. The Brutalist-evoking Buckner Building once housed one thousand troops, a cinema, bowling alley, shooting range, church and more. This gargantuan building was a city in and of itself. Today, it sits discarded, like a concrete apparition from war's past.

Opposite, top: Viewing Whittier's ex-Army buildings from the ferry; **bottom**: the abandoned Buckner Building

FIRST-TIME TIPS

Check ahead for the Anton Anderson Memorial Tunnel's opening times. This is a one-lane tunnel that alternates directions and type of transport (car versus train).

....

Book ahead if you plan on spending the night – accommodations are few and far between and fill up quickly.

....

Bring waterproof clothing and gear – inclement weather is never far away.

....

The former US Army Headquarters is now a museum; the lobby of BTI (Begich Towers Inc), Whittier's main apartment building, also holds a fascinating photo gallery.

AMAZING CROWD-FREE EXPERIENCES

Explore the Sound's wildlife and blue-veined glaciers. Lazy Otter Charters (lazyottercharters.com) runs wonderful half- and full-day wildlife and glacier-viewing trips around the Sound, limited to just six passengers.

Walk the Whittier Army Port Historical District. Imagine a once-bustling US Army outpost on a self-guided walking tour of Whittier's historic installations.

Paddle your way around Blackstone Bay. Sea kayaking trips in this cinematic bay offer a chance to see actively carving and tide-water glaciers.

Get invited to a house party. Check out how locals live (nearly all of them!) at BTI (Begich Towers Inc), once Alaska's largest apartment building when it opened as the Hodge Building in 1956.

Feast on scrumptious Alaska salmon burgers. Dine at Wild Catch Café, one of the best of Whittier's short list of waterside dining options.

Escape to Lu Young Park. This small tucked-away park is a tranquil place to see wildlife and mountain vistas.

GETTING THERE

Fly into Ted Stevens Anchorage International Airport. From there, Whittier can be reached via a stunning 90-minute car ride along the Turnagain Arm and Portage Valley, by ferry with the Alaska Marine Highway (dot.alaska.gov/amhs) from Cordova and Valdez or on the Alaska Railroad (alaskarailroad.com), which travels to Whittier as part of its Glacier Discovery service.

WHEN TO GO

July

Prince William Sound is bound by a temperate rainforest, so drizzle is a near-constant presence, but July is unquestionably the driest month of the year.

Wai'anae Coast Hawaii

TEEMING WILDLIFE AND RICH HAWAIIAN HISTORY SET THIS REMOTE STRETCH OF COAST APART

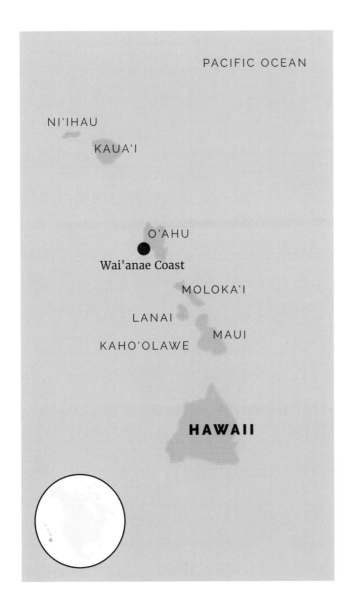

PACIFIC OCEAN

NI'IHAU

KAUA'I

O'AHU

Wai'anae Coast

MOLOKA'I

LANAI

MAUI

KAHO'OLAWE

HAWAII

The Wai'anae Coast – literally, 'water of the mullet,' thanks to its rich fishing grounds – is the exact opposite of Honolulu. It's a place of quiet remoteness, no crowds and miles of wild coastline. The further north you venture, the wilder the coastline.

Rural towns are home to tightly knit communities that cling to traditional Hawaiian values and heritage. Rich in culture, some of O'ahu's most significant archaeological landscapes are located in the valleys here; there are even petroglyphs carved into the sandstone. Unfortunately, economic oppression, commercial exploitation and gentrification have long plagued the area, so it's important to tread lightly along this coast and travel with a respectful attitude.

About an hour drive from Waikīkī, the leeward side of the island is home to plenty of hiking trails, wild dolphins and beaches (with plenty of elbow room) where snorkeling is superb. From December to May, it's possible to see migrating humpback whales passing through. And turtles and reef fish are around all year.

GO IF YOU LIKE...
- 💜 *dolphins*
- 💜 *coastline*
- 💜 *nature*
- 💜 *dreamy vistas*
- 💜 *farm life*
- 💜 *hiking*

Why go to the Wai'anae Coast?

The biggest draw on this rugged coast is nature. Be a citizen scientist for the day and *mālama ke kai* (care for and protect the sea) with Wild Side Specialty Tours, a company that runs sustainable tours focused on photography, marine education and snorkeling.

Back on land, put hiking high on the agenda; there are plenty of trails to choose from. If you don't have much time on your hands, opt for the Mā'ili Pillbox Hike (aka Pu'u O Hulu Trail, aka Pink Pillbox Hike). The 2-mile (roundtrip) trail is dotted with military bunkers that served as lookouts during World War II. Another quick trek is the moderately challenging Lahilahi Point Trail. For a more strenuous trek, try 4000-foot Mount Ka'ala, the tallest peak on the island. The 6-mile (roundtrip) hike crosses boardwalks, goes up steep ridges and finishes in a cloud forest.

Opposite: Exploring lush forests along the Pink Pillbox Hike

GETTING THERE

The best way to get to the Wai'anae Coast is by car. From the Daniel K Inouye International Airport, it's about an hour's drive. Take into account that there is one road in and one road out; traffic can be bad during rush hour or if there is a brush fire. Alternatively, you can take TheBus (Rte 401).

WHEN TO GO

Nov – Apr

Weather is consistently dry and sunny thanks to the mountain range that typically keeps the rain away. To see humpback whales, visit from November through April. January through March is considered peak season for the whales.

AMAZING CROWD-FREE EXPERIENCES

 Picnic at Kaena Point State Park, a remote and mostly untouched wilderness. Look for Hawaiian spinner dolphins, Hawaiian monk seals and sea birds.

 Volunteer at Kahumanu Organic Farms and Cafe to help get fresh produce out to the community and enjoy a farm fresh meal at the cafe. Proceeds support local families in need.

 Dine on poke nachos and mahi mahi by the sea at the Beach House by 604. Stay for live music and sunset.

 Stroll by the Ko Olina Lagoons for sunset or take a dip. The four lagoons are great for newbie snorkelers because they're protected from the open ocean.

 Hang ten on gentle waves at Pokai Bay with West Side Surf Lessons. If surfing isn't your thing, they rent stand-up paddleboards, boogie boards and kayaks.

 Swim at Maili Beach Park during the summer months when the water is calm to check out the coral reef. Have reef-safe sunscreen handy.

FIRST-TIME TIPS

Be *cautious and polite* when exploring. Don't go beyond signs that say kapa (keep out). Don't leave valuables in your car. Break-ins have been known to happen here.

....

Support local businesses. This is a chronically underfunded community; remember that locals are understandably skeptical of travelers.

....

Be alert while driving along *Hwy 93 (Farrington Hwy)* as it's narrow and winding. Accidents are common.

....

By law, you must *stay 50 feet away from monk seals* and 50 yards from spinner dolphins.

....

Winter-time waves can be gnarly; *check the surf report.*

Opposite: Aerial views of
Hālawa Valley

Moloka'i Hawaii

UNSPOILED NATURE AND FLOURISHING CULTURE ON HAWAII'S FRIENDLY ISLE

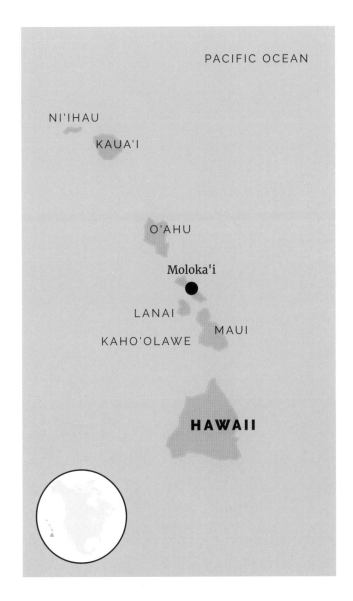

PACIFIC OCEAN

NI'IHAU

KAUA'I

O'AHU

Moloka'i

LANAI

MAUI

KAHO'OLAWE

HAWAII

Moloka'i is the heart of Hawaii – and not just geographically. The fifth-largest Hawaiian Island, Moloka'i is only 38 miles long and 10 miles across at its widest point, but it's home to many superlatives: the tallest sea cliffs in the world, the state's longest fringing reef, Hawaii's longest stretch of sandy beach... And despite being part of an island chain that's one of the most popular visitor destinations in the world, Moloka'i has managed to maintain a small-town vibe that has earned it the nickname the Friendly Isle.

But Moloka'i isn't for everyone. There are no traffic lights here, no luxury resorts, no nightclubs, and no big-box retailers or chain restaurants. You won't sip a fancy mai tai topped with *liliko'i* foam at a trendy bar or indulge in a luxurious facial at a world-class spa. You may not even get consistent cell service. But what you will experience is an unspoiled paradise, with empty golden-sand beaches, peaceful native rainforests filled with endangered honeycreepers and languid days that make you feel like you're actually on vacation.

GO IF YOU LIKE...
- *sea cliffs*
- *secluded beaches*
- *quiet nights*
- *uncrowded hikes*
- *Hawaiian culture*
- *native birds and plants*

Why go to Moloka'i?

There's a wooden sign just outside the Moloka'i Airport that reads, *Aloha. Slow down. This is Moloka'i.* That's not a suggestion. The island's seven thousand residents aren't keen on rushing, and they expect visitors to take it easy, too. Explore the many hiking trails, across rugged sand dunes or through a pristine old-growth rainforest, or lounge on one of many stunning beaches – you'll likely be the only one there.

Native Hawaiian culture flourishes here, with many families growing taro, managing fishponds and dancing hula. The dozens of fishponds that dot the coastline are among the best preserved in the state (though many are in disrepair). From Kalaupapa to Hālawa Valley, emerald-green sea cliffs rise to almost four thousand feet above the ocean. It's believed that here, in lush Hālawa Valley, ancient Polynesians settled as early as 650 CE. And when you see the breathtaking beauty of this classic cathedral valley, you'll understand why.

GETTING THERE

Only one commercial airline – Mokulele Air, operated by Florida-based Southern Airways – flies to the state-run airport. It provides nonstop service from Oahu, Maui and Hawaii Island in nine-seat Cessna planes that fly low and slow. Getting around requires a car. There's a couple of car rental options, one taxi service (molokaitaxi.com) and no public transportation. Ridesharing service is extremely limited.

WHEN TO GO

May – Oct

In Hawaii, the rainy season ends around May and summer weather – daylong sunshine, cooling trade winds – extends into early winter. While summer is often the busiest time for travel to the state, Molokai only gets between 25 to 30 visitors a day.

AMAZING CROWD-FREE EXPERIENCES

 Decorate and mail an actual coconut at the Hoolehua Post Office. Call ahead (808-567-6144) to see if there are coconuts available.

 Explore the 921-acre Moomomi Preserve. The rugged coastal area, with dunes shaped by trade winds, boasts more than 22 native Hawaiian plant species.

 Drive to Hālawa Valley past ancient Hawaiian fishponds and Kaluaaha Church. Swim at Hālawa Beach Park or book a guided hike (halawavalleymolokai.com) to the secluded Mooula Falls.

 Visit Kalaupapa National Historical Park (nps.gov/kala), established in 1980 to preserve the experiences of patients with Hansen's disease who were forced into exile here.

 Visit Molokai Plumerias (molokaiplumerias. com) in Kaunakakai, where you can tour the farm, pick fragrant flowers and string a lei.

 Hike to a rare montane bog on the slopes of Kamakou Preserve high in the mountains. More than 90% of its plant life is found nowhere else in the world.

Opposite, left to right: Delicate kukui nut flowers; stepping into the rainforest; this lesser-visited island embraces a slow pace.
Above: Hālawa Valley

Wailuku Hawaii

TAKE A DEEP DIVE INTO ART AND CULTURE IN THIS SMALL TOWN

At the base of the West Maui Mountains sits Wailuku: a historic town free of the tourist traps and crowds of Maui's most popular sights. It's a place where aunties take the *keiki* (children) to art class, locals line up for that morning cup of java and music lovers young and old come to listen to live tunes. Wander the streets in search of public murals or head out of town to ʻĪao Valley State Monument, where King Kamehameha I defeated Maui's army in an effort to unite the Hawaiian islands in 1790.

If you're wondering if you should vacation on Maui in light of the devastating wildfires that ripped through Lahaina in August 2023, the answer is yes. Except for Lahaina, Maui is open for business and locals are welcoming travelers with open arms. With an economy supported almost completely by tourism, visiting – in a mindful and sustainable way – is a powerful way to boost the island's small businesses and help Maui heal. Wailuku is about 20 miles east of Lahaina.

GO IF YOU LIKE…
- ♥ *street art*
- ♥ *organic eats*
- ♥ *bohemian vibes*
- ♥ *mom-and-pop shops*
- ♥ *island-inspired music*
- ♥ *bento boxes*

Why go to Wailuku?

Wailuku is refreshingly Old Hawaii. Full of businesses that have been passed down through generations – funky coffee shops, boutiques, wooden storefronts, old churches – it offers a glimpse into the past mixed with a boho vibe. The town's street murals, created by artists from around the world, have spurred a cultural renaissance over the past decade and cemented its status as a creative canvas.

Stay for a few days at family-owned ʻĪao Valley Inn for dreamy views of the ʻĪao Needle, and tour the family-run Mahina Farms Maui, where fostering community and culture is the guiding principle. Visitors learn about Hawaiian plant medicine, traditional arts and the moon calendar. Hop over to the Maui Arts and Culture Center in Kahului for comedy acts and concerts by local and international musicians. The Ukulele Festival is a solid choice and outdoor movie nights are the perfect family outing.

GETTING THERE

Fly into Kahului Airport. From there, it's an easy 10-minute drive to Wailuku, or you can take a rideshare or taxi. There is a designated parking lot at Wells Park within walking distance of the town and free street parking with a two-hour limit. Da Bee Shuttles take people around town; pick-up is at the Maui Lani Safeway parking lot.

WHEN TO GO

Year-round

There's really no bad time to visit Wailuku. January through March is the rainy season, but showers don't last long. Mid-December through mid-April is considered the peak season.

FIRST-TIME TIPS

Get up early in the morning to find piping-hot malasadas (Portuguese donuts) before they all sell out.

....

Download the Hoʻokamaʻāina app for three free walking tours. Choose from cultural, historic and public art themes. Along the way, you'll see native plants, the Kaʻahumanu Church and the Bailey House Museum.

....

For the best snapshots of the street murals, go early when cars aren't parked in front of the walls.

....

Watch kiteboarders and windsurfers propel themselves into the air at Kanahā Beach Park and Kaʻa Point, thanks to the consistent winds on this side of the island.

Left: Colorful downtown Wailuku.
Opposite, left: Kite surfing at Kanaha Beach; **right**: Nakalele Blowhole's dramatic jet

AMAZING CROWD-FREE EXPERIENCES

 Take a dip in the cool stream that flows through ʻĪao Valley State Monument, and stroll through the botanical garden. You'll need to reserve an entrance slot.

 Deep dive into Hawaiian history at Hale Hōikeike at the Bailey House, which showcases cultural artifacts and contemporary work.

 Zipline through Maui Tropical Plantation in Waikapū, nosh on crab cakes and sautéed mahi mahi at Cafe O'Lei and buy local products (*liliko'i* jam and banana bread) at Kumu Farms.

 Snack on sugar-dusted, pudding-filled pastries at Four Sisters Bakery. Opened in 1983, the bakery is named after the daughters of the Filipino couple who started the business.

 Catch a show at the Spanish mission–style Īao Theater, built in 1927 and listed on Hawaii's Register of Historic Places. It stages a wide range of musicals.

 Find one-of-a-kind Hawaiian handicrafts at Native Intelligence. They stock everything from koa calabashes to lauhala hats, all made on Maui.

Whidbey & Camano Islands Washington

THE SMALL-TOWN CHARMS OF TWO NEIGHBORING ISLANDS MAKE FOR AN IDYLLIC WEEKEND GETAWAY

Whidbey Island is the larger of the two, measuring 55 miles in length and up to 12 miles across, making it the fourth-longest island in the US and the largest in Washington.

Though varying in size, both islands are home to thriving art communities. Each has dozens of art galleries, art walks and studios that are open all year long. History also is an important draw, as both islands were backdrops to significant moments in the nation's military history.

However, the main attraction will always be the islands' lush green landscapes, cool blue waters and slow and simple vibe.

GO IF YOU LIKE...
- ♥ *a slower pace*
- ♥ *pristine nature*
- ♥ *artistic getaways*
- ♥ *local crafts*
- ♥ *coastal adventures*
- ♥ *military fortifications*

Nestled in Puget Sound, Whidbey and Camano Islands beckon travelers with their unspoiled beauty and easy-going charm. These serene destinations offer a refreshing escape from the hustle and bustle of nearby Seattle and other more popular islands like the San Juans. With gorgeous landscapes, rich history and welcoming communities, these islands deserve to be at the top of every traveler's offbeat bucket list.

Why go to Whidbey and Camano Islands?

Whidbey and Camano Islands make the perfect weekend getaway for art lovers, history buffs, outdoor enthusiasts and families. No trip to the islands would be complete without visiting a few galleries, and the islands make a point for community and art to coincide in the form of performance arts and regular events.

Whidbey Island is home to Fort Casey State Park – one of a trio of strategically placed fortifications defending the entrance to the Puget Sound built in the early 20th century. Though never used to defend an enemy attack, Fort Casey was used as a training facility up to the mid-1940s.

Though the islands' art scene and history add to their charm, nothing can compare to their natural beauty. Deception Pass State Park, Cama Beach State Park and Fort Ebey State Park are all must-sees.

FIRST-TIME TIPS

Rent a car or drive your own. _Having a car is ideal_ for exploring the islands at your pace.

....

Traveling midweek is best to avoid the long weekend ferry lines and tourist traffic. Ferries are first come, first serve, so purchasing a ferry ticket in advance isn't especially useful as it doesn't guarantee you a spot.

....

Savor the fresh seafood and locally produced treats for an authentic culinary experience.

....

Embrace the weather. _Pack layers and rain gear_ to stay warm and dry.

....

Get a Discover Pass. It's your ticket into the islands' state parks.

AMAZING CROWD-FREE EXPERIENCES

 Witness majestic orcas and humpback whales frolicking in the Salish Sea. Local pods of orcas can often be seen in late spring, summer and early fall around the islands. Bring binoculars if you want to do some serious whale-watching from shore.

 Hike the scenic trails and check out the iconic Deception Pass Bridge. If you're not content with seeing Deception Pass from land, book a boat tour with a company like Deception Pass Tours, which offers summer tours that focus on the history and nature of the area.

 Browse the galleries and studios showcasing regional artists.

 Enjoy kayaking, fishing, and camping on the islands' peaceful shores.

 Unravel the islands' history by touring the well-preserved Fort Casey. Guides are sometimes available to offer additional information and stories about the history of the cannons and the fort itself.

 Discover historic lighthouses that once guided sailors along the rugged coastline.

GETTING THERE

The easiest way to get to Whidbey Island is by ferry. From Seattle, take the Clinton ferry in Mukilteo. If traveling from further north, cross Deception Pass Bridge. From the peninsula, the Coupeville ferry in Port Townsend is best. Camano Island shares several of these routes, though most travelers opt for the Camano Bridge.

WHEN TO GO

May – Sep

In line with typical Pacific Northwest weather, the islands reach peak season in the late spring and summer. To beat the summer crowds, go in early fall when the weather is still cooperating.

Clockwise from top left: Admiralty Head Lighthouse; campfire stories on Whidbey Island; Fort Ebey State Park

Opposite: Snowy Mount Adams rising above the wheat fields of Washington

Goldendale Washington

STARS, RODEOS AND STONEHENGE IN SOUTH-CENTRAL WASHINGTON

Goldendale rarely comes to mind when travelers are planning a trip to the Pacific Northwest. Located in south-central Washington, about 120 miles northeast of Portland and 220 miles southeast of Seattle, it's not a place that is on the way to many other destinations.

However, a trip to this small town is worth the extra mileage. Goldendale is home to one of the largest and most accessible public telescopes in the United States. Hundreds of stargazers travel here every year to greet the stars at Goldendale Observatory State Park. Observing the celestial sights is almost as thrilling as taking in the historical ones. In addition to the Observatory State Park, Goldendale also is home to its own full-scale replica of Stonehenge – the nation's first WWI memorial, dedicated in 1918.

Like most cities in southern Washington, Goldendale's culture is steeped in its agricultural history. With robust 4H programs, high-school rodeo clubs and three Northwest Professional Rodeo Association rodeos every summer, ropers, riders and the curious are well catered to.

GO IF YOU LIKE...
- *peaceful escapes*
- *art museums*
- *unique historical sites*
- *stargazing*
- *boutique wineries*
- *rodeos*

Why go to Goldendale?

The Goldendale Observatory's main telescope was built by four amateur astronomers in the 1960s. In 1973, the founders selected Goldendale as the telescope's home not only because of its low light pollution, but also because the town had been the site of an important albeit unsuccessful experiment in 1918 to prove Einstein's theory of relativity during a total solar eclipse. The founders knew that another eclipse was coming to the area in 1979, and wanted to be prepared.

Another tie-in with history is the Stonehenge Memorial, located near the Maryhill Museum of Art. It was erected as the nation's first WWI memorial and dedicated to the fallen soldiers of Klickitat County by Maryhill Museum of Art founder, Samuel Hill. The art museum itself has more than 80 works by Auguste Rodin, Native American crafts, Orthodox icons and unique chess sets in its collection.

GETTING THERE

To reach Goldendale, visitors can fly to Portland International Airport in Oregon. From there, it's a scenic two-hour drive along I-84 and through the Columbia River Gorge National Scenic Area.

WHEN TO GO

Apr – Oct

Goldendale tends to have less precipitation and higher temperatures than western Washington. June through August are the hottest and most popular months to visit. To beat the tourist season, visit in spring or early fall.

FIRST-TIME TIPS

Renting a car is ideal for exploring the area at your pace.

Go wine tasting. Goldendale is part of the Columbia River Gorge wine region, and there are several top vineyards nearby. Maryhill Winery and Waving Tree Winery are the two most famous wineries.

Pack essential hiking gear, including sturdy shoes and weather-appropriate clothing.

Make lodging reservations before arriving in Goldendale. Most campgrounds require advance reservations, especially from May to September.

Get a Discover Pass, which will provide entry to Goldendale Observatory State Park.

Opposite: Full-scale Stonehenge replica near Maryhill . **Left:** Meadows filled with purple lupines; **right**: Goldendale Observatory Interpretive Center

AMAZING CROWD-FREE EXPERIENCES

Marvel at the majestic Maryhill Stonehenge and view an extensive Native American collection and a permanent Rodin sculpture exhibit at the Maryhill Museum of Art.

Visit Goldendale Observatory State Park and observe celestial wonders through telescopes at one of the nation's best stargazing spots.

Traverse the scenic Klickitat Trail. Enjoy hiking or cycling along the former railroad tracks, surrounded by stunning landscapes.

Explore the beauty of Columbia Hills Historical State Park. Hike to see petroglyphs and revel in the panoramic views of the Columbia River Gorge.

Unwind at Maryhill Winery. Savor award-winning wines and take in breathtaking views of the vineyard and Mt Hood.

Wander through charming streets lined with antique shops, galleries and local eateries in historic downtown. Gunkel Orchards Fruit Stand, a family-owned fruit stand featuring fresh handpicked cherries, apricots, peaches and grapes, is a local favorite.

Opposite: Oregon's mineral-streaked Painted Hills

John Day Region Oregon

CENTRAL OREGON'S DIVERSE BIOSPHERE TAKES CENTER STAGE

WASHINGTON

John Day Region

OREGON

IDAHO

CALIFORNIA

NEVADA

The chunk of central Oregon known as the John Day Region gives visitors unparalleled opportunities to explore an incredible variety of landscapes, all in a single weekend. At its heart sits John Day Fossil Beds National Monument, with three separate units: the Painted Hills, Clarno and Sheep Rock. Each is distinctive, with miles of hiking trails and a window into a different geological time period. Heading south brings you into the dense pine forests and high-desert terrain of the Ochoco National Forest. A leisurely drive north by northwest leads to

the buttes, mountains and rolling hills of the Umatilla National Forest.

Visitors to the John Day Region can experience winding canyons reminiscent of the Southwest, lush old-growth forests similar to coastal Oregon, high desert plains reminiscent of Big Sky country and geological oddities almost Martian in appearance. And nestled amidst it all are gorgeous towns with restaurants, brewpubs, museums and curio shops. Given its tremendous scenic diversity, it's a bit surprising that John Day retains such an offbeat character.

GO IF YOU LIKE...
- 🖤 *panoramic vistas*
- 🖤 *surreal scenery*
- 🖤 *local history*
- 🖤 *quirky towns*
- 🖤 *paleontology*
- 🖤 *hiking*

Why go to the John Day Region?

You'd need to visit every state west of the Rockies to experience the breadth of terrain encompassed in the John Day Region. Though the otherworldly mustard yellow and burnt umber landscape of the Painted Hills feel like a world away from the lush greens of the Ochoco National Forest, the entrances to both are less than 20 miles from the town of Mitchell.

Travelers with an interest in the history of the American West will find no shortage of opportunities to learn about the past in the area's museums. And for those who prefer to measure history in geological terms, the Thomas Condon Visitor Center in the national monument's Sheep Rock Unit has extensive displays of the terrain, flora and fauna of the region dating back to the Cretaceous period. It's also a working laboratory center where visitors can watch paleontologists work with fossils in real time.

GETTING THERE

Most visitors driving from Portland take I-84 through the Columbia River Gorge before heading south into the region. It's a four-hour drive to Mitchell. Rte 26 skirts the Ochoco National Forest and is popular with bicyclists. Grant County Transportation (grantcountypeoplemover.com) runs buses between Bend and Prairie City three times a week.

WHEN TO GO

Apr – Oct

Spring and fall have the best weather. Late spring and early summer is when the wildflowers bloom, making this already colorful region a veritable kaleidoscope. Summers are popular, but hot and dry. Carry plenty of water.

Opposite: Iron, mudstone and manganese oxide form bands of color at the Painted Hills Unit

AMAZING CROWD-FREE EXPERIENCES

 Float on the John Day. Oregon's longest undammed river has sandy beaches, glorious meadows and plenty of spots for boating and white-water rafting.

 Step into a cultural time capsule. The Kam Wah Chung Heritage Site commemorates 19th-century Chinese immigrants Ing 'Doc' Hay and Lung On. Tours are held hourly.

 Dig for fossils. The hill behind Wheeler High School in the town of Fossil is a designated public fossil-hunting site for amateur paleontologists. Admission is $5.

 Party in Mitchell. Besides being ideally situated for local exploration, this hip town has two annual festivals and is home to the fabulous Tiger Town Brewpub.

 Stock up on books. Charming Canyon City is home to DGDriscoll's, an independent secondhand book store with a maze of shelves.

 Have a slice of pie. Also in Canyon City, Squeeze-In is a locally beloved restaurant serving excellent meals (gluten-free available), awesome shakes and pastries.

FIRST-TIME TIPS

Camping is prohibited inside John Day Fossil Beds National Monument, but there are plenty of privately operated <u>campgrounds and RV parks</u> located in the region. Mitchell, Dayville and Fossil are the closest towns to the park entrances with food and lodging.

....

Resist the temptation to skip any of the three designated Painted Hill units – each has markedly diverse colors and scenery, and each unit has <u>multiple hiking trails</u> ranging up to 2½ miles in length.

....

<u>Cell phone service</u> is sporadic outside of most towns and nonexistent when driving through the canyons. Enjoy your digital detox!

Wallowa County Oregon

SCENIC VIEWS AND FRONTIER VIBES IN THE PACIFIC NORTHWEST'S ALPINE BACKYARD

WASHINGTON

Wallowa County

OREGON

IDAHO

CALIFORNIA

NEVADA

In the summer months, Wallowa attracts folks from Portland, Boise and beyond seeking art, activities and scenic beauty. Take the time to visit and you'll soon understand why coastal Cascadians from Portland to Seattle fondly refer to Wallowa County as the Alps of the Pacific Northwest. With summits that are lower than 10,000 feet and none of the glaciers of the Cascades, this may seem like hyperbole, but the Wallowas do not lack for steep, dramatic peaks.

Most of Wallowa's skiing is in the backcountry meaning it's experts only, but an escape from the crowds of other Oregon resorts is all part of the appeal.

In the Rocky Mountains, people searching for the mountain days of yore have been flocking to Montana. In the Pacific Northwest, meanwhile, that same quest for a quiet, inexpensive, outdoorsy home draws the intrepid to Wallowa County. If you're looking to save your citified soul, the snowcapped mountains, acres of forest and endless opportunities for hiking, cycling, fishing and backcountry skiing here will definitely do the trick.

GO IF YOU LIKE...
- ♥ *alpine scenery*
- ♥ *hiking*
- ♥ *biking*
- ♥ *rafting and kayaking*
- ♥ *backcountry skiing*
- ♥ *untrammeled nature*

Why go to Wallowa County?

Wal'alwa, as the area is called by the local Nez Perce, the original inhabitants of the region, is eastern Oregon's most temperate county; as such, it's long been a beloved summer destination for urban Cascadians. Snowmelt-fed Wallowa Lake is bracingly cold on the hottest summer days, and the many rivers running through the county provide excellent opportunities for rafting, kayaking, swimming and fishing.

Visitors looking for a laid-back town experience will love exploring Joseph. Over the last decade this unpretentious spot on Wallowa Lake's northern end has become home to urban artisans of all stripes, resulting in a Main St teeming with art, boutiques, restaurants, bars and venues. For a town whose official population barely cracks 1200, it's an impressive assembly. You can easily spend a full day checking out the shops here – make your first stop the community-run Josephy Center for Arts and Culture, a nonprofit offering classes and exhibits.

Opposite, clockwise from top: Wallowa's Barn Tour; criss-crossing streams in the Wallowa Mountains; downtown Joseph

© BOB POOL / SHUTTERSTOCK, © LARRY GEDDIS / ALAMY STOCK PHOTO, © CSNAFZGER / SHUTTERSTOCK

FIRST-TIME TIPS

Take the time to *explore towns along the way*. Elgin has a charming Old West vibe and a historic opera house. Stop by Cowboys and Angels for an amazing homecooked meal.

....

Learn about the tribe who call the area home at the *Nez Perce Wallowa Homeland Visitor Center* in the town of Wallowa.

....

Lostine is home to a multibuilding thrift store with curios dating back to the 19th century.

....

County seat *Enterprise* has excellent restaurants and bars. Terminal Gravity is renowned for craft beer and live music on the lawn.

AMAZING CROWD-FREE EXPERIENCES

Dance barefoot in the grass. At the century-old Wallowa Lake Lodge, expect gourmet meals, live bands and a beautiful lakeside lawn suitable for dining and dancing.

Support local artisans. The lively Wallowa County Farmer's Market attracts artists, musicians and farmers from around Oregon.

Cycle Wallowa's paved roads, where gorgeous mountain views await around every bend. Mountain bikers can also get their fix on challenging climbs and windy singletrack.

Hear the call of the wild. Zumwalt Prairie is home to wildlife including bobcats, deer, black bears, gray wolves and elk.

Enjoy serious seclusion. The luxurious Minam River Lodge, accessible only by plane, horseback or an 8.5-mile hike, is an excellent place to get away from it all.

Go for the bronze. Wallowa has a number of talented sculptors whose work can be admired throughout the county and purchased at Parks Bronze and TW Bronze Foundry in Enterprise.

GETTING THERE

Make no mistake – the Wallowas are out there. Tucked into the northeast corner of Oregon, the town of Joseph (the northern Wallowas) is roughly equidistant from Boise (four hours), Spokane (four hours) and Portland (five hours). The western Wallowas, accessed from La Grande, just off I-84, are a bit closer. Rte 82 runs between La Grande and Joseph.

WHEN TO GO

May – Oct

Though winter activities abound for the intrepid, most visitors to the Wallowa-Whitman National Forest come during the summer; Rte 82 can be treacherous during the winter months.

Butte Montana

BIG SKY COUNTRY WITH MINING HISTORY, CAVE TOURS AND MYRIAD WAYS TO EXPLORE

CANADA

MONTANA

Butte

IDAHO

WYOMING

other museums in town provide additional context.

Butte is also a great place for outdoor recreation. It's located near the Continental Divide National Scenic Trail – which runs all the way to Mexico – and has easy access to numerous trailheads. Around 40 miles away, Lewis and Clark Caverns State Park offers cave tours for a subterranean adventure, as well as hiking and biking trails, camping and more. Eighteen miles east of Butte, the Ringing Rocks showcase the area's unique geology – they make chiming noises when tapped just right with a hammer.

GO IF YOU LIKE...
- *mining history*
- *quirky B&Bs*
- *museums*
- *outdoor recreation*
- *spelunking*
- *skiing*

Butte was once dubbed 'the richest hill on earth' and this southwestern Montana city was well-known for its rich ore deposits, in particular copper. Visitors can descend 100 feet underground on a tour of the Orphan Girl Mine at the World Museum of Mining or spend time exploring the extensive Butte–Anaconda Historic District to learn even more about the area's past. The Mai Wah Society Museum provides insight into the community's Asian heritage, and several

Why go to Butte?

Butte was one of the filming locations for the *Yellowstone* prequel *1923*, so fans might notice a few familiar locations around town. It also offers several interesting historic lodging options. The Copper King Mansion was built in the 1880s for William A Clark, one of the town's wealthy 'Copper Kings.' Tour the historic structure – which is now a bed and breakfast – or spend the night. The 12-room Miner's Hotel is a boutique property in a historic bank building. Sleep in the old vault – now transformed into a room – and visit the below-ground speakeasy.

After you've learned all about Butte's history, be sure to get outside. Go for a hike on the Continental Divide Trail, try out mountain biking, pitch a tent or get a license and go hunting or fishing. Winter also provides plenty of opportunities for outdoor fun, with options like downhill or cross–country skiing, snowmobiling and more.

GETTING THERE

Butte is located near the intersection of I-90 and I-15, and visiting on a road trip is a great way to see the town. If you're traveling by air, tiny Bert Mooney Airport is just outside Butte and has flights to Salt Lake City. The regional airports in Bozeman (80 miles east) and Missoula (120 miles northwest) serve a larger number of destinations.

WHEN TO GO

Jun – Oct

Summer and fall are the best times to visit Butte. Many attractions are seasonal, so be sure to check operating schedules and plan accordingly.

FIRST-TIME TIPS

Download the free Story of Butte self-guided tour (storyofbutte. org) and learn as you explore the historic district and beyond. The site already includes more than a dozen tours and hundreds of stories.

Some tours and attractions require advance bookings, so be sure to check.

Butte abounds with historical sites, but don't miss the outdoor recreation opportunities just a short drive from town. Make some time to hit the trails – this is Big Sky country after all. Be sure to take bear safety precautions: it's bear country, too!

AMAZING CROWD-FREE EXPERIENCES

Take a Butte Mule Tour on a five-passenger side-by-side 'mule' for a peek into the past.

Explore the Continental Divide Trail, which runs through Montana near Butte. Several trailheads near the city provide easy access.

Enjoy hiking, mountain biking and horseback riding in Thompson Park, which has 25 miles of trails and is managed by the US Forest Service.

Visit Lewis and Clark Caverns State Park for popular cave tours, then get out on the park's 10 miles of trails.

Peer into Berkeley Pit, an old open-pit copper mine 7000 feet long and 1600 feet deep – though it's now filling with water.

Visit the memorial for the Butte Warehouse Explosion of 1895, a tribute to those who perished in the conflagration at Kenyon Connell Warehouse.

Clockwise from top left: The Cathedral Room in Lewis and Clark Caverns; the Copper King Mansion; historic headframes on Butte hill

93

River of No Return Idaho

ANIMALS REMAIN KING IN IDAHO'S PRISTINE SWATHE OF WILDERNESS

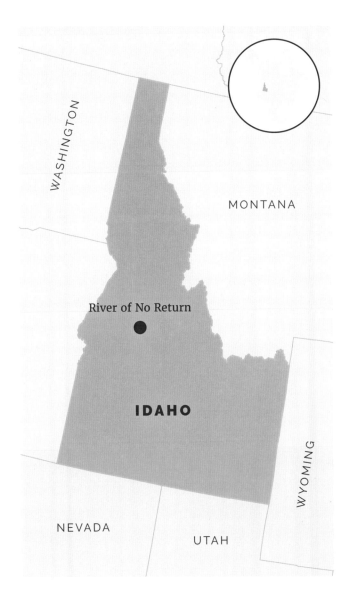

MONTANA

WASHINGTON

River of No Return

IDAHO

NEVADA

UTAH

WYOMING

Spread over 2.3 million acres of mountainous terrain, Idaho's Frank Church–River of No Return Wilderness is the second-largest contiguous wilderness area in the continental US.

At its heart is the Salmon River. Originally dubbed the 'River of No Return', – early pioneers found it nearly impossible to navigate – this 485-mile waterway is one of the longest free-flowing rivers in the United States. There are no dams here, few roads and even fewer people. It's a little slice of heaven that starts its course from the rugged Sawtooth Mountains and cuts straight through the middle of a vast region filled with toothy crags and evergreens.

Rafting is the number one draw. On the Middle Fork of the Salmon you'll find waters so clear, you'd think you were gliding over a Caribbean reef. Lower down on the Main Salmon, you get bigger waves, steep walls and plenty of wildflowers.

Wherever you go, expect primitive hot springs, fabulous backpacking and amazing wildlife, including the area's signature resident, the bighorn sheep.

GO IF YOU LIKE...
- 💜 *white-water rafting*
- 💜 *hot springs*
- 💜 *backpacking*
- 💜 *wildlife watching*

Why go to the River of No Return?

Every year, more than 90 million people visit national parks like the Great Smoky Mountains, the Grand Canyon and Zion.

But up here, under the broad, arching Idaho sky, only 10,000 people per year are afforded the once-in-a-lifetime opportunity of floating the Middle Fork of the Salmon River – a river canyon that's so deep it actually surpasses the depth of the Grand Canyon. With so much space and so few people, you can actually hear the silence.

Apex predators abound – bears, wolves, lynx and wolverines – as do lumbering ungulates, like elk, moose and bighorn sheep. Nearly every day you have a chance of spotting a bald eagle.

If rafting isn't your thing, the wilderness also has about 2600 miles of maintained trails that spiderweb across the mountains and meadows, cross burbling streams and raging rivers and take you to remote lakes and spiraling peaks.

Below: Launching rafts on the Salmon River. **Opposite**: A young bull moose cools off

FIRST-TIME TIPS

The best adventures require several days of paddling or hiking. <u>Allow at least a week.</u>

....

Stop to talk to people. At <u>Buckskin Bills</u>, along the Main Salmon, you'll find artifacts from a true mountain man who called this area home.

....

<u>Dress warmly.</u> Getting caught in a torrential summer rainstorm is no joke. Luckily, there's almost always a hot spring nearby.

....

As a nationally designated wilderness, there are a number of requirements for everything from packing out trash to your scat. <u>Respect and honor this wilderness area.</u>

GETTING THERE

Bozeman Yellowstone International Airport is the closest major airport to the northeast side of the wilderness area, and is a four-hour drive from the offbeat town of Salmon. Boise Airport is a bit closer to southern access points like Challis, and is also a four-hour drive. Commercial rafting operations like Oars offer guided trips on the Middle Fork and Main Salmon.

WHEN TO GO

Jun – Aug

Summer comes late in these northern latitudes. You'll find great weather from June through August, with easier access to a wilderness that rests under a blanket of snow all winter long.

AMAZING CROWD-FREE EXPERIENCES

 Raft the hard-to-reach Selway River. While the Salmon is the main attraction, the equally beautiful Selway River also gets its start here.

 Travel from lake to lake in the Bighorn Crags. This rugged cirque has dozens of pristine alpine lakes and snow-crusted peaks. Fishfin Ridge can be reached on a day hike.

 Drop a line in gold medal waters. There are 23 species of fish here. Practice catch-and-release to protect the steelhead trout and Chinook salmon.

 Spend an afternoon soaking in a hot spring. Get away from the crowds in riverside retreats along the Salmon River.

 Travel in the off-season. Take on a backcountry skiing adventure to find a connection with nature that may transform your life forever.

 Look up. The area has some of the clearest skies imaginable. Receiving the top rating on the Bortle scale as an 'excellent dark-sky site,' you can see the cosmos in its greatest splendor.

Opposite: Wyoming's
mighty Wind River
Mountain Range

Lander Wyoming

OUTDOOR ADVENTURE WITH A SPLASH OF HISTORY

MONTANA

WYOMING

Lander

COLORADO

The town was established in 1884
and incorporated in 1890, and is
considered to be 'where the rails
end and the trails begin,' since
the Cowboy Line of the railroad
ended here in 1906. Explore the
Museum of the American West
or Fremont County Pioneer
Museum to learn more, and
head to South Pass City State
Historic Site to tour venerable
structures and try panning for
gold. Lander is also near the
Wind River Reservation, which
is home to the Eastern Shoshone
and Northern Arapaho tribes
and encompasses 2.2 million
acres. Check windriver.org for
upcoming powwows and cultural
events open to the public.

GO IF YOU LIKE...
- *mountains*
- *hiking*
- *backpacking trips*
- *climbing*
- *fishing*
- *Western history*

Lander is the gateway to Wyoming's Wind River Mountains – a
spectacular range that entices hikers, climbers, fly-fishers and
other outdoorsy types. While less visited than the Tetons, the Wind
Rivers include Wyoming's highest summit – Gannett Peak, which rises
to 13,804 feet – as well as another 40 mountains also over 13,000 feet
tall. Sinks Canyon State Park is just a few miles from town and is popular
with climbers, hikers and mountain bikers.

Why go to Lander?

Recently named a Continental Divide Trail Gateway Community (together with South Pass City), Lander is the perfect place to access far-flung outdoor adventures whether by hiking, backpacking, climbing or biking. It's considerably less busy than other outdoor recreation hubs in the region, namely Wyoming's Grand Teton National Park and Colorado's Rocky Mountain National Park, both of which see millions of visitors each year. Much of the Wind River Range is located in the Bridger-Teton and Shoshone National Forests, which has abundant wildlife, lakes and glaciers.

In Sinks Canyon State Park, go for a hike and be sure to check out the Sinks, which is where the Middle Fork of the Popo Agie River dips underground before reemerging at the surface about a quarter of a mile downstream. Climbers flock to Sinks Canyon State Park and other climbing areas, such as Wild Iris, near Lander. In winter, try cross-country skiing and snowshoeing.

GETTING THERE

Driving is the best way to reach Lander. Central Wyoming Regional Airport is 30 miles away in Riverton, and regional hubs Rock Springs, Casper and Jackson have additional flight options. Just over four hours away, Salt Lake City is the largest international hub in the area.

WHEN TO GO

Jun – Sep

Summer and fall are ideal for outdoor activities, though be sure to check snow levels in the high country before making your early summer plans.

FIRST-TIME TIPS

Even if you spend most of your time on the trails, be sure to stop by some of Lander's stellar eating and drinking establishments like Gannett Grill, Lander Bar, Lander Brewing Company and Cowfish.

....

Consider hiring a guide or outfitter, especially if you're short on time. They can help you find the best fishing spots or guide your backcountry adventure.

....

Not sure about conditions in the backcountry or where the fish are biting? Stop by a local outdoor shop to learn the latest.

....

In the Wind River Mountains, be prepared for mosquitoes, especially early to mid-season.

AMAZING CROWD-FREE EXPERIENCES

 Hike, bike, climb or camp at Sinks Canyon State Park, which has the famous Sinks where the Popo Agie River disappears underground.

 Spend a weekend or more on a backcountry adventure in the Wind River Mountains, home to Wyoming's tallest summit, 13,804-foot Gannett Peak.

 Visit South Pass City State Historic Site, a gold-mining town established in 1867. Visitors can join seasonal tours or go panning for gold.

 Learn about the area's history at the Fremont County Pioneer Museum, packed with interesting stories on local characters, like the nation's first female justice of the peace, Esther Hobart Morris.

 Pedal the mountain biking trails at the Alpine Science Institute and Johnny Behind the Rocks, which is about 15 miles from town.

 Plan your visit for the International Climbers' Festival in July, to enjoy clinics, comps, demo gear, volunteer opportunities, meet-ups, yoga, art, film and more.

Clockwise from top: hiking the Wind River Mountains; climbing the Cirque of the Towers; Carissa Saloon in South Pass City

Dead Horse Point Utah

A HOME BASE IN BETWEEN TWO OF UTAH'S MOST POPULAR PARKS

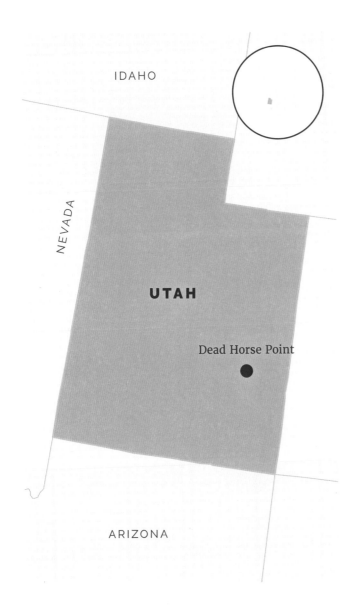

IDAHO

NEVADA

UTAH

Dead Horse Point

ARIZONA

Southeastern Utah enchants visitors with its striking canyons, arches and desert landscapes, and Canyonlands and Arches National Parks are two of the most popular destinations in the state. But what if you want to experience red-rock country without bumper-to-bumper park traffic? Consider setting up camp at Dead Horse Point State Park, which features spectacular canyon views and puts you in close proximity to a number of sights in the Moab area.

There are several stories about the origin of Dead Horse Point's unusual name. According to one, turn-of-the-century cowboys used the park's secluded mesa as a natural corral for wild mustangs, taking advantage of the steep cliffs to fence in the most valuable horses. One time, however, the horses were abandoned, and they wound up dying of thirst on the desolate mesa top.

Today, the park is an excellent option for those looking for a little bit of peace in a well-trafficked part of Utah, and offers hiking trails, scenic viewpoints, dark skies and access to some fabulous mountain biking.

GO IF YOU LIKE...
- 💚 *Arches National Park*
- 💚 *Canyonlands National Park*
- 💚 *red rock hiking*
- 💚 *desert camping*
- 💚 *mountain biking*
- 💚 *canyon views*

Why go to Dead Horse Point?

Dead Horse Point soars above the rocky expanse in between Canyonlands and Arches. A scenic drive along Rte 313 leads to the small state park, which is perched on a mesa top overlooking the Colorado River, two thousand feet below.

Hikers, mountain bikers and birders will love the inspiring trails that skirt the canyon's rim. These routes connect to several scenic points, providing visitors with an up-close glimpse of the region's diverse plant and animal life. They're a hardy group, as the high mesa only receives 10 inches of rain per year.

But the most amazing experience of all comes at sunset. Once you've snagged a spot at one of the campsites, make your way to Dead Horse Point itself. As day fades into dusk, watch as the sun paints the distant canyons in hues of yellow, orange and red, before fading into soft evening pastels.

GETTING THERE

Dead Horse Point State Park sits midway between Arches National Park and Canyonlands National Park's Island in the Sky entrance. It's a thirty-minute drive to Moab proper. Moab has a small regional airport with connections to Denver and Salt Lake City, though most people drive here via I-70.

WHEN TO GO

Apr & May, Sep & Oct

Spring and fall are the best times to visit. School holidays make summer the peak season, but be warned: the desert is scorching hot. Winter brings snow, freezing temperatures and fewer crowds.

FIRST-TIME TIPS

Dry heat can really sneak up on you. Always have at least <u>a gallon of water</u> available, though you may need more in summer.

Beat the heat by <u>covering up</u>, not stripping down. Light, breathable layers will keep the sun off your skin.

<u>Parking at the point is limited</u>, especially at sunset; if you're camping in the park, just walk or bike there instead.

If a road calls for a <u>4WD vehicle</u>, don't take the rental sedan.

A fall here is almost always fatal, so <u>skip the selfie</u> and steer clear of the edge.

AMAZING CROWD-FREE EXPERIENCES

 Pack a telescope to take advantage of Dead Horse Point's dark skies.

 Stay in one of the park's yurts for a more comfortable camping experience. Nothing beats waking up and walking onto your porch for views of the canyon beyond.

 Use Dead Horse Point as a springboard for exploring other offbeat sights, including Thelma and Louise Point, accessible from the Moab entry of the Shafer Trail.

 Rent a mountain bike from Bighorn Mountain Bike near the park's entrance. They also offer guided tours.

 Bring your watercolors and set up at sunrise or sunset for an unforgettable plein air painting experience.

 Wake up before the sun and make the quick drive to Arches National Park. You'll be able to admire the views of its arches at sunrise and make it back to Dead Horse Point before the crowds arrive.

Above: Partition Arch in Arches National Park; **below:** dark sky camping in Dead Horse Point

Grand Junction Colorado

COLORFUL SPRINGBOARD TO HIGH-DESERT HIKING, BIKING AND WINE TASTING

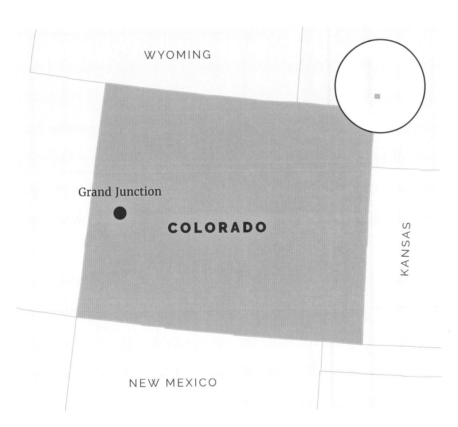

WYOMING

COLORADO

Grand Junction

KANSAS

NEW MEXICO

But hidden behind the farms and 24-hour gas stations is a charming little town in the high desert, a place rich in beauty and outdoor activity – from wine tasting and picking your own lavender to dramatic red rock hikes and some of the best singletrack mountain biking in the state. Best of all, the region is conveniently compact; most of its sights and activities are located just a few miles apart, making it possible to have a full day of fun without having to spend half of it in your car.

GO IF YOU LIKE...
- ♥ *Moab*
- ♥ *desert hiking*
- ♥ *wine tasting*
- ♥ *mountain biking*
- ♥ *rock climbing*
- ♥ *dinosaurs*

Grand Junction is one of Colorado's long-time agricultural hubs, its first orchards planted in the 1880s – almost immediately after the Indigenous Ute were pushed out by the US Army. Sitting along I-70 just 30 miles from the Utah border, it's often thought of as no more than a convenient pitstop to flashier destinations in Moab or the Colorado Rockies: a place for gas, coffee and the state's famous Palisade peaches, if they're in season.

Why go to Grand Junction?

Grand Junction is off the radar for most tourists – at least for now. A burgeoning destination, its charming downtown is dotted with quirky boutiques and bustling cafes, while the streets are decked out in murals and sculptures. Nearby, Las Colonias River Park has newly developed riverfront trails plus great paddling and tubing. And a clutch of new hotels – Camp Eddy with its souped-up Airstreams and the sleek Hotel Maverick – make GJ a comfortable basecamp. Beyond town you'll find myriad outdoors options, many of which you'll have to yourself. The red rock wonderland of Colorado National Monument is the heavy hitter with trails, climbs and epic drives. Colorado wine country in Palisade is a close second. And there's more: wild mustang reserves and dinosaur digs, desert bike rides and farm tourism. Not bad for a place most people think of as just a highway pitstop!

GETTING THERE

The quickest way to Grand Junction is to fly. The city is home to western Colorado's largest airport, though most flights serve Denver International Airport. Flying directly to Denver is certainly cheaper, but it also means driving four to five hours on the increasingly busy I-70. Riding the train from downtown Denver is a scenic and sustainable alternative, but it takes about eight hours.

WHEN TO GO

Sep – Nov

Autumn brings mild temperatures, sunny days and brilliant fall colors, making outdoor activities particularly pleasant. This is also grape harvest season, and the local vineyards are bustling with activities and special events.

FIRST-TIME TIPS

Rent a car to explore the greater Grand Junction region; public transportation is limited to town.

....

Carry a refillable water bottle to *stay hydrated* in this desert playground. On trails, one gallon of water per person per day is recommended.

....

Mountain bikes, e-bikes and cruisers are available to rent in downtown Grand Junction and nearby Fruita and Palisade.

....

Hire a pedicab to go wine tasting in order to avoid driving or even pedaling between vineyards.

....

Most restaurants close by 8 or 9pm; for late-night eats, try the chains near the highway.

Opposite, left: Peach blossoms beneath Mount Garfield; **right**, woolly alpacas at SunCrest Orchard. **Above:** Sculpted sandstone at the Rattlesnake Arches

AMAZING CROWD-FREE EXPERIENCES

Backcountry camp in Colorado National Monument, with spectacular red rock vistas during the day and dark starry skies at night – not to mention hiking and all levels of rock climbing.

Hike Rattlesnake Canyon in McKinnis Canyons NCA, a spectacular 12.4-mile hike past nearly three dozen natural arches – the most in the US outside Arches National Park.

Spot wild mustangs at Little Book Cliffs, a 36,000-acre reserve of craggy canyons, home to one of the country's last protected bands of wild horses.

Join paleontologists from the Museums of Western Colorado on a half- or full-day dig in the Mygatt-Moore Quarry, where thousands of dinosaur bones have been unearthed.

Follow the 25-mile Fruit and Wine Byway in Palisade, stopping to taste wines and peaches, pick lavender and even trek with alpacas.

Mountain bike on the Kokopelli Loops Trail, a ruggedly beautiful high-desert ride.

Alamosa Colorado

LOW-KEY FARM TOWN WEDGED BETWEEN HIGH PEAKS AND SERENE WILDLIFE REFUGES

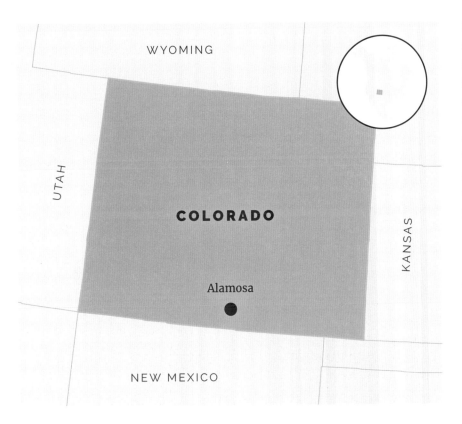

Situated on the banks of the Rio Grande and nestled at the foot of the shark-tooth Sangre de Cristo mountains, Alamosa has an unbeatable setting. It's home to roughly 9800 residents, over one-third of whom are students. Thanks to its location – the valley still retains some of its original wetlands – this is a great spot for birding: numerous migratory species pass through in spring and autumn.

Though nature is the big draw in the San Luis Valley, the coffee shops, boutiques and restaurants in Alamosa's historic downtown make for a great Colorado base camp.

GO IF YOU LIKE...
- *bird-watching*
- *sand dunes*
- *hiking*
- *small towns*
- *UFOs*
- *craft beer*

Colorado's most famous mountain resorts – we're looking at you, Vail and Aspen – bustle with tourists all year long. That translates into pricey accommodations, long lift lines and trailheads overflowing with cars. But the Centennial State has so much more to offer. Take the San Luis Valley, for example. Giant sand dunes and UFO sightings add a touch of weird to this high-altitude agricultural community, which is anchored by the under-the-radar charms of small-town Alamosa.

Why go to Alamosa?

Many travelers pass through Alamosa on their way to visit Great Sand Dunes National Park or climb the Sangres, but this multicultural community is worthy of more than just a quick pitstop.

Alamosa is sandwiched between two federally protected wilderness areas – Alamosa National Wildlife Refuge and Monte Vista National Wildlife Refuge – and their wetlands serve as an important haven for both migratory birds and larger animals, like beavers and coyotes. Nearby Zapata Falls, accessible via a short hike, is a stunning 25-foot waterfall tucked into a narrow canyon. If Mother Nature is not cooperating, do a little shopping downtown, sip a craft beer at one of the breweries or catch a performance by the Creede Repertory Theatre.

And, of course, don't forget Great Sand Dunes National Park. Not only does it protect the tallest sand dunes in North America, this is also one of the quietest places in the country.

FIRST-TIME TIPS

If you visit in March or April, you'll see nearly 20,000 sandhill cranes as they fuel up during their northward migration.

Alamosa sits at 7544 feet above sea level. At this elevation, altitude sickness is common, so drink lots of water and take it easy for the first few days while you acclimate.

Even at the height of summer, overnight lows can dip into the 40s. Pack warmer layers for the mornings and evenings.

Keep an eye out for (and maintain a respectful distance from) porcupines, which like to snooze in the trees along the Rio Grande.

AMAZING CROWD-FREE EXPERIENCES

 Observe wildlife. Grab your binoculars and camera, then head to Alamosa National Wildlife Refuge or Monte Vista National Wildlife Refuge.

 Wander the waterfront. Stroll the Rio Grande Trail and enjoy views of the river, the Sangre de Cristo Mountains in the distance and golfers hitting the links at Cattails Golf Course.

 Sip craft beers. Order a pint at one of Alamosa's many craft breweries, including the Colorado Farm Brewery and the San Luis Valley Brewing Company.

 Shop for treasures. Peruse the wares of Alamosa's antique shops and boutiques, including Hunt Avenue Boutique, Wild Roses, Treasure Alley and Green Spot.

 Learn about the Utes and the early Hispanic settlers who have long called this valley home at the San Luis Valley Museum.

 Take a scenic drive. Traverse the Los Caminos Antiguos Scenic Byway to immerse yourself in the region's history, culture and natural beauty.

Above: Pin-drop silence at North America's tallest sand dunes

GETTING THERE

Fly into Denver International Airport in Colorado or Albuquerque International Sunport in New Mexico, rent a car and hit the road. From Denver, the roughly 230-mile drive south takes about four hours – skip the interstate and follow Hwy 285 for the most scenic route. From Albuquerque, it's a slightly shorter journey, at just 3½ hours.

WHEN TO GO

Jun – Aug

Summer is the best season for fresh produce and outdoor recreation in the San Luis Valley, with highs in the low 80s. It's also ideal weather for sipping a flight of craft beers on a sunny patio.

Opposite: Kelp forests beneath the waves

Channel Islands National Park California

ENCOUNTER WINDSWEPT HILLS AND SWAYING KELP FORESTS AT AN UNSPOILED ARCHIPELAGO

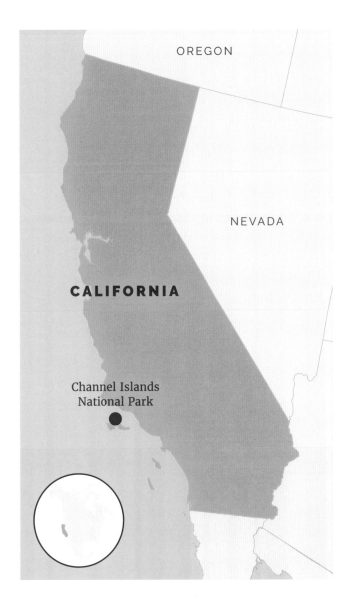

OREGON

NEVADA

CALIFORNIA

Channel Islands
National Park

Imagine the oak-pocked landscape of coastal southern California as it looked when only the Indigenous Chumash and Tongva people lived here in harmony with the seasons and ocean rhythms. It's actually possible to imagine such a time at Channel Islands National Park, about a dozen miles offshore from the south-facing coastline between Santa Barbara and Ventura.

Sometimes referred to as the 'Galápagos of North America' for its biodiversity, the islands' marine and terrestrial species number over two thousand. The most emblematic of these is the endemic island fox, a housecat-sized canid with no natural predators and thus a delightfully blasé attitude toward human visitors (who average over 300,000 annually).

The islands are worth a visit any time of year – for springtime wildflower blooms, whale migrations and spectacular diving and snorkeling. Depending on the island, you can have a near-solitary backcountry camping experience or a guided kayak tour through sea caves and over thriving kelp forests.

GO IF YOU LIKE...
💚 *sea kayaking*
💚 *whale-watching*
💚 *hiking*
💚 *camping*

Why go to Channel Islands National Park?

Trips to the Channel Islands pack a lot of punch, even for travelers who only have a day to spend. The boat ride across the channel is itself a wildlife-watching opportunity, with harbor seals and common dolphins making almost guaranteed appearances. From late spring to early fall, humpback and blue whales migrate through the channel, while gray whales move through from November to April.

Once you've made landfall, hiking the trails through arid island interiors to stunning bluff-top overlooks afford dramatic views down rugged coastlines and out to neighboring islands. Or get on the water, paddling a kayak around the island's outer edge, exploring sea caves like the colorful Painted Cave and getting a look at life in the kelp forests. The visibility and rich biodiversity makes for excellent diving and snorkeling – look for bright-orange garibaldi (California's state marine fish) or a lucky sighting of a giant black sea bass.

GETTING THERE

Island Packers Cruises (islandpackers.com) runs year-round trips to Santa Cruz and Anacapa Islands. Trips to the outer islands of Santa Rosa, San Miguel and Santa Barbara Islands are seasonal. Almost all trips launch from Ventura Harbor, 67 miles north of LA. Trips to Santa Cruz Island take from one to 1½ hours, while the journey to Santa Barbara Island takes around three hours.

WHEN TO GO

Aug – Oct

The peak season begins to wind down in August, with fewer crowds and more reliably warm and sunny weather. Though the ocean tends to be calm during the fall, hot Santa Ana winds may whip up the swell.

© BLUEBARRONPHOTO / SHUTTERSTOCK. © LUIS RAMIREZ / 500PX / GETTY IMAGES

Opposite, left: Curious native island foxes; right, sea cliffs of Anacapa Island. Above Mountains rising out of the Pacific Ocean

FIRST-TIME TIPS

Bring everything you'll need, including water, even on day trips. Potable water is available only at Scorpion Canyon campground on Santa Cruz and Water Canyon campground on Santa Rosa.

Dress in layers, as island weather can change quickly, and take measures to prevent seasickness: conditions can be rough in the Santa Barbara Channel.

Keep it pristine and pack all your trash off the island.

Weekdays are less crowded during the peak summer season.

Check the NPS website (nps.gov/chis) for current closures, and confirm and reserve boat passage before reserving a campsite.

AMAZING CROWD-FREE EXPERIENCES

 Head to the less-visited outer islands during the open season. The vast majority of visitors travel to Santa Cruz, the most easily accessed.

 Paddle the island's fringe on a guided kayaking tour with Channel Islands Adventure (islandkayaking.com) to get up close to freestanding arches, sea caves and ocean denizens.

 Go on a snorkel or dive to immerse your senses in the island's marine universe. Its cold crystalline waters are home to vibrant, colorful sea life amid the swaying kelp.

 Make tracks along island trails, where you're likely to see an island fox or two as you traverse windswept hills and valleys, coastal bluffs and secluded beaches.

 Fully soak in the island magic by backcountry camping on Santa Cruz or a more remote outer island; advance planning is required.

 Charter a private kayaking, snorkeling, hiking or combo trip and experience the islands with your own posse.

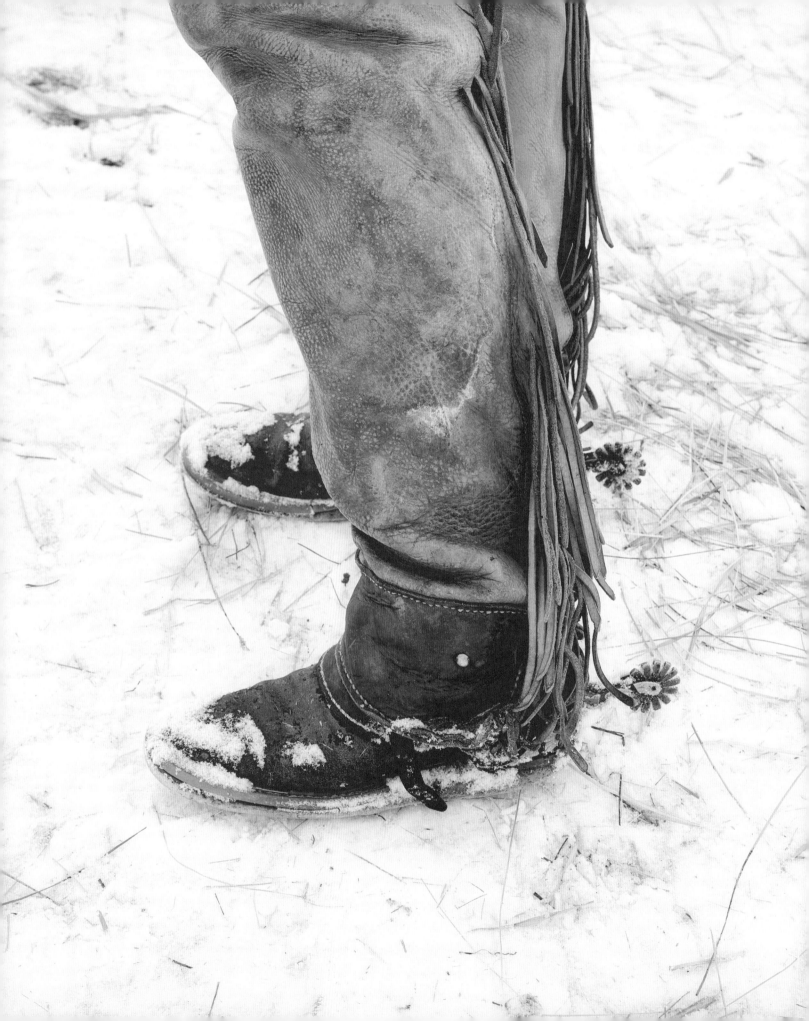

Elko Nevada

NO LONGER THE END OF THE LINE

IDAHO

Elko

NEVADA

UTAH

CALIFORNIA

ARIZONA

Elko has always been a place for life's high-plains drifters, and railroad tycoon Charles Crocker named the town for the awkward grazers who still roam the nearby hills. Its Basque culture, dating back to the Nevada Territory's sheepherding heyday, remains firmly rooted in festivals and food. You never walk away hungry from a Basque repast.

But Elko has not entirely escaped the 21st century: a hip brewpub competes with ginmills of lesser repute along Railroad Ave, and you're likely to meet some of the modern-day venturers trying their luck in the gold and silver mines of the nearby hills.

GO IF YOU LIKE…
- ♥ *cowboy culture*
- ♥ *wide-open spaces*
- ♥ *Basque culture*
- ♥ *public art*
- ♥ *elk*
- ♥ *railway lore*

The heart of America's Great Basin is Elko, Nevada, which sits at an elevation of 5066 feet. Back in 1868, Elko was the end of the line for the nascent Central Pacific Railroad, and its aging engines dot the downtown in a homage to the railway's golden age. Halfway between Reno and Salt Lake, you can still step off of Amtrak's California Zephyr at 11th and Water Sts and enter a slice of the Old West.

Why go to Elko?

Wide-open spaces. Elko and its environs hold an average of three people per square mile, so you'll have plenty of breathing room here. There's no shortage of hiking, jogging and biking trails in the nearby mountains, as well as fishing opportunities in pristine trout-stocked alpine lakes.

The summer months host the nation's largest Basque party, a major ballooning festival with dirigibles filling the skies like multicolored candies, and a series of bike and road races, including one that combines humans, bikes and burros.

Birders will be pleasantly surprised by the six Audubon-designated Important Bird Areas in the surrounding Jarbidge, Ruby and Goshute Mountains; one of the largest annual migrations of raptors passes overhead in the autumn. Golden and bald eagles soar majestically over the sere landscape, and the Rubies are the only place in the United States to see an exotic Himalayan Snowcock.

GETTING THERE

Amtrak's California Zephyr gets you to Elko from any point between Chicago and San Francisco; Greyhound bus lines have even more options from the West. It's a three-hour drive west across the salt flats from Salt Lake City, from where there is also an irregular puddle-jumping flight. In town, e-scooters using the Bird app are fun and convenient.

WHEN TO GO

Jul – Sep

July and August have the best weather, a range of festivals from Basque to rodeos and optimal wildlife viewing.

FIRST-TIME TIPS

You might need time to <u>acclimate to the altitude</u>. Don't forget the sunscreen, hat and sunglasses.

. . . .

Don't skip the <u>Western Folklife Center</u> honoring the cowboy lifestyle, or the shops that can kit you out head-to-toe in vaquero duds.

. . . .

The <u>Star Hotel</u> and other Basque eateries will stuff you to the gills with delicacies like pork loin or lamb shank, generously heaped with red peppers and diced garlic.

. . . .

Centered around the Pioneer Saloon's 19th-century mahogany and cherrywood bar, February's <u>Cowboy Poetry Gathering</u> heralds the oldest of traditions – the wayfaring poet and minstrel – and its unique expression in the American West.

Opposite: Cowboy poetry and open mic nights at Stockmen's Casino. **Above, left:** Backcountry hiking in the Ruby Mountains; **right:** Elko's Old West aesthetic

AMAZING CROWD-FREE EXPERIENCES

 Hike, bike or run the Rubies, 'Nevada's Swiss Alps,' with lung-busting inclines and crystal-clear lakes.

 Explore the ghost towns left behind when the mining boom went bust and the silver spurs and Pony Express stations disappeared.

 Stroll downtown, admiring the artistic expression in the Artwalk murals and Centennial Bootwalk, a collection of six-foot-high multicolored boot statues evoking equal parts Earp (Wyatt) and Elton (John).

 Visit a working ranch with cowboy John Collett, who will regale you with tales of runaway cattle, and even take you to see Nevada's own renegade wild mustangs.

 Mount a stallion or snowmobile at the Cottonwood Ranch and meander through the mountain streams and gullies for spectacular views of wildflowers, sagebrush and wildlife.

 Listen to cowboy lingo at January's Poetry Gathering; there are large crowds by Elko standards, but some readings are in surprisingly intimate venues.

Opposite: Secluded shores along the Alpine Lakes Loop

Great Basin National Park Nevada & Utah

STARGAZING AND SCENIC DRIVES IN AN OTHERWORLDLY NATIONAL PARK

one of the country's least-visited national parks, recording less than 150,000 visits in 2022.

But solitude seekers have other reasons to visit this desert-and-mountain treasure, which is earning kudos on the astrotourism circuit. Time your visit for stargazing talks, the Astronomy Festival and rides on the seasonal Star Train. Atop Wheeler Peak, hikers pass bristlecone pines that are among the oldest trees in the world. Underground, stalactites, stalagmites and rare shield formations fill the colossal Lehman Caves.

GO IF YOU LIKE...
- 💜 *Yosemite National Park*
- 💜 *Kings Canyon National Park*
- 💜 *stargazing*
- 💜 *cavern tours*
- 💜 *historic trains*
- 💜 *scenic drives*

Pygmy rabbits. Dark rangers. The Prometheus Tree. Mythical creatures in a fantasy novel or sights you'll encounter in Great Basin National Park? Anchored by Wheeler Peak in the far eastern fringes of Nevada, Great Basin National Park is about as remote as you can get in the Lower 48. From the city of Fallon outside Reno, it's a 320-mile drive east on the Loneliest Road, a two-lane highway stretching across the sunbaked center of Nevada to the park. Las Vegas is three hundred empty miles south. By the numbers, Great Basin is

© ARLENE WALLER / SHUTTERSTOCK

123

Why go to Great Basin National Park?

Evening light pollution is almost nonexistent here. This means the cosmos can be observed in its full celestial glory at night. From nearby Ely, the Nevada Northern Star Train climbs a mountain ridge for the sunset then stops for telescope-assisted stargazing. Park rangers – dubbed Dark Rangers – lead the tours. Rangers also lead astronomy programs Wednesday, Friday and Saturday nights in summer atop Wheeler Peak. The park has five developed campgrounds, which means you can also admire the cosmos from your own campsite.

At the base of the peak, two ranger-led tours – the Lodge Tour and the Grand Palace Tour – spotlight various speleothem formations in Lehman Caves. Plans are finalizing for two additional tours in 2024: a short highlights tour and a three-hour wild tour with off-trail adventuring in the caves. For cool digs, book a room at the revamped Stargazer Inn in the town of Baker beside the park.

GETTING THERE

The national park, which is located in Nevada near the Utah state line, is three hundred miles north of Las Vegas. Salt Lake City International Airport, the closest major airport, is 235 miles northeast. The park is easily accessed from I-15 and US 50. There is no public transportation, and you'll need a car to explore once you arrive.

WHEN TO GO

Jun – Aug

The park is open year-round. Summer is best for hiking, with many trails crisscrossing lofty Wheeler Peak and the Snake Range. Cross-country skiing is fantastic in winter. The temperature in Lehman Caves is a constant 50°F regardless of the season.

Opposite: Knotty bristlecone pines are the world's oldest living trees

AMAZING CROWD-FREE EXPERIENCES

 Drive 12 miles to the 13,065ft summit of Wheeler Peak. The narrow road twists through different ecological zones as it climbs the mountain, which rises dramatically from the Great Basin Desert.

 Hike past ancient bristlecone trees and a rapidly receding glacier – the only one in Nevada – on the 4.8-mile round-trip Bristlecone and Glacier Trails.

 Fish for brown, brook, rainbow and cutthroat trout in Lehman and Baker Creeks after obtaining your Nevada fishing license.

 Pitch your tent in the backcountry off Snake River Rd for solitude and unfettered communion with the starry cosmos above Wheeler Peak.

 Explore quirky sights along the Loneliest Road, officially known as US 50, including a singing sand dune, Pony Express stations and a famous shoe tree.

 Admire Lexington Arch, a six-story limestone arch at the end of a 3.6-mile round-trip hike off unpaved Lexington Rd. Check the park website for road conditions and parking in this remote area.

FIRST-TIME TIPS

Lower Lehman Creek Campground is open year-round. The other developed campgrounds are typically open May through October. Sites at four campgrounds are reservable from June through August at recreation.gov.

Make a reservation for _Lehman Caves_ tours, which regularly sell out in summer. Star Train tours, which also sell out, run from June through early September.

Cell phone service in the park can be spotty and there is _no public wi-fi._

The park _does not have a gas station_ though you can fill up 24/7 at the Sinclair station in Baker. You'll have to drive at least 30 miles to reach a charging station.

This spread:
Bisti Badlands, New Mexico

Southwest
USA

Opposite, top: Vintage gas pumps on Erie St; **bottom**: Bisbee's arty downtown

Bisbee Arizona

A MINING TOWN THAT CONFOUNDS EXPECTATIONS WITH ECLECTIC ART AND CUISINE

Wedged into Tombstone Canyon in the sunbaked emptiness of southeastern Arizona, Bisbee and its scrubby surrounds aren't exactly eye candy. And that's without mentioning the monstrous open-pit mine gaping skyward at the end of town. But take a closer look. Like the best offbeat destinations, Bisbee flips your expectations.

Old Bisbee evokes the early 20th century with its sturdy brick buildings packed tight along Main St. These historic structures were built during the city's prosperous copper mining years. Today, they are abuzz with up-to-the-minute art galleries, innovative restaurants and an eclectic array of inns. During the Depression, the Works Progress Administration built thousands of concrete steps along the mining trails climbing the slopes of the surrounding canyon. Murals now brighten these alleyways, transforming downtown into one big gallery. Beyond Old Bisbee, you can wander goblin-like hoodoos, sleep in a vintage Airstream and poke around lonely Erie St – the heart of a mid-century mining community. As for the citizens, well, you'll soon discover a quirky yet appealing joie-de-vivre that amps up the charisma.

GO IF YOU LIKE...
- *Jerome*
- *Tucson*
- *Santa Fe*
- *art*
- *quirky towns*
- *mining history*

Why go to Bisbee?

The art will surprise you in Bisbee. The Bisbee Arts and Culture District encapsulates almost the entire downtown, where murals, galleries, museums and craft shops are plentiful and eclectic. Open since 2019, the Artemizia Foundation's museum and galleries north of downtown are a wonder. A passion project of artist and philanthropist Sloane Bouchever, the foundation displays an extraordinary collection of contemporary pieces by a global array of modern masters. Displaying an exuberant collection of offbeat found art, the Broadway Stairs Art Gallery downtown is an outdoor collection of thrift-store finds as well as a community improvement project – meaning anyone can contribute.

A short drive from the city drops you in the immersive history of Fort Bowie State Park and the fantastical rocks of Chiricahua National Monument. These intriguing parks are about as offbeat and remote as you can get in the Southwest.

FIRST-TIME TIPS

Time your visit for the end of the week or the weekend. Many shops and restaurants are closed Monday through Wednesday.

For a communal art experience, stroll downtown the second Saturday of the month during the After Five art walk.

The 'scenic viewpoint' on Hwy 80 overlooks an enormous open-pit copper mine that shut in 1974. Impressive, yes. Scenic, no.

To catch the last daily reenactment of the shootout at the OK Corral in Tombstone, leave Bisbee by 2:15pm for the 30-minute drive. The last show is at 3pm. There will be crowds.

AMAZING CROWD-FREE EXPERIENCES

 Stroll shops, galleries and alleyways along Main Street in downtown Bisbee.

 Admire contemporary, graffiti and street art – Picasso, de Kooning, Banksy, Annie Leibovitz – at the Artemizia Foundation. Visits are by a 60-minute tour. Book ahead.

 Learn the story of copper mining in Bisbee at the Bisbee Mining and Historical Museum. Mine-train tours inside the nearby Queen Mine are pretty cool, but get crowded.

 Drive 90 minutes to Seussian spires, pinnacles and boulders at Chiricahua National Monument.

 Hike into history at Fort Bowie National Historic Site where a 1.5-mile loop trail provides a well-rounded analysis of the Apache Wars.

 Spend the night in an Airstream at the Shady Dell, where trailers are outfitted with hip decor from the Golden Age of car travel.

GETTING THERE

Your best bet is to travel to Bisbee by car. The town is about 50 miles south of I-10 off exit 303. The town of Tombstone and its famed OK Corral are 25 miles north and the Mexican border is 10 miles south. Tucson International Airport is 90 miles northwest.

WHEN TO GO

Mar – May

The temperature is generally pleasant in spring, with average highs in the 70s and 80s. Spring also sees the least amount of rain. Bisbee is a mile high in the mountains, so it's typically cooler than Tucson.

Above: Adobe ruins at Fort Bowie National Historical Site; **left**: The yawning Lavender Pit copper mine

131

New Mexico

SURREAL LANDSCAPES, ATOMIC BOMBS, ANCIENT HISTORY AND OUTLAWS

It's the fifth-largest state in the country, and New Mexico has stretches of road where you can drive for hours without seeing more than a handful of cars. There are ancient ruins from Ancestral Puebloans (whose descendants still live in the state's 19 Pueblos), crumbling ghost towns reminiscent of silver boom days gone by, saloons peppered with bullet holes, military research facilities that changed the world, UFO crash sites and chile-laden cuisine. Get out of your car in certain spots and you might think you've landed on Mars.

New Mexico isn't just the Land of Enchantment. It's the land of What the Heck Was That!?

GO IF YOU LIKE...
- 🤍 *Southwest cuisine*
- 🤍 *UFOs*
- 🤍 *Pueblo history and culture*
- 🤍 *green chiles*
- 🤍 *ghosts*
- 🤍 *stargazing*

To be sure, New Mexico has plenty of touristy hotspots. Santa Fe and Taos get their share of art lovers and outdoorsy adventurers, Albuquerque has its balloons and Breaking Bad fans, and the big-ticket national parks like Carlsbad Caverns and White Sands see over a million visitors annually. But if you're not afraid of a long-distance road trip, then this quirky place becomes a galaxy to discover.

Why go to New Mexico?

The thing with New Mexico is that crowds buzz around a handful of destinations while leaving the rest open for exploration. For instance, the parking lot at Bandelier National Monument gets so busy that the National Park Service had to implement a molasses-slow shuttle service, but Santa Clara Pueblo's Puye Cliff Dwellings up the road have informative Indigenous guides and are way less touristy. And though Chaco Canyon has some of the oldest ruins in the United States, the hikes are better in the otherworldly and less-visited landscapes of the Bisti/De-Na-Zin Wilderness Area.

In 2023, New Mexico hit cinema screens with *Oppenheimer*. See where the Manhattan Project happened in Los Alamos, then stay the night to stargaze at the Dark Sky Park in the 89,000-acre Valles Caldera National Preserve. It's always worth seeing what's going on (and taking home sustainability tips) at the Earthships in northern New Mexico, as the groundbreaking eco-community continues to expand worldwide.

FIRST-TIME TIPS

Keep an eye on the news for <u>wildfires</u>. The state that gave birth to the real Smokey the Bear is no stranger to forest fires, including the devastating Calf Canyon/ Hermits Peak fire in 2022.

....

New Mexico has well-paved highways, but the driving can get dicey on backroads, especially in the Four Corners region. Make sure you have <u>four-wheel drive</u> and high clearance, and check ahead if roads are passable.

....

New Mexico's <u>19 Pueblo communities</u> often host traditional dances, powwows and markets. Check the annual calendar to see which events that are open to the public.

AMAZING CROWD-FREE EXPERIENCES

 See where the first atomic bomb was invented in Los Alamos and subsequently detonated at the Trinity Site near White Sands National Park.

 Look for aliens in the Martian landscapes of the Bisti Badlands/De-Na-Zin and Ah-Shi-Sle-Pah Wilderness Areas and UFO remnants in the desert around Roswell.

 Explore the dozens of ghost towns that crashed with the railway and silver booms before they're completely lost to the elements, including Chloride, Mogollon, Madrid and Cimarron.

 Follow Billy the Kid's footsteps to hotels and saloons peppered with bullet holes, and go to Lincoln where the infamous bandit escaped from jail.

 Visit fascinating Mogollon cliff dwellings in Gila National Forest and Puye cliff dwellings in Santa Clara Pueblo, both of which are little visited.

 Camp under the stars at Cosmic Campground, the state's only Dark Sky Sanctuary, as well as in New Mexico's seven Dark Sky Parks.

GETTING THERE

Fly into the international airport in Albuquerque or the regional one in Santa Fe. Or get your kicks with a slow-and-steady road trip from Arizona or Texas on old Route 66. If coming from Colorado, it's all aboard the Cumbres and Toltec steam train south to Chama in northern New Mexico.

WHEN TO GO

Sep – Nov

Avoid New Mexico's summer crowds by visiting in the fall. Bonus: it's green chile harvest season.

Above: Ancient Puebloan caves at Gila Cliff Dwellings; **left:** The ghost town of Mogollon

Tulsa Oklahoma

CULTURAL CENTER WITH MIDWESTERN CHARM AND ART DECO STYLE

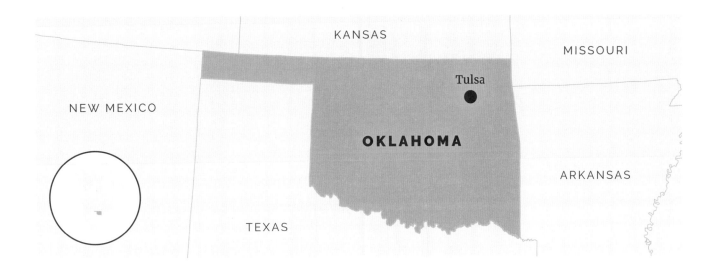

The self-proclaimed oil capital of the world since the early 1900s, Tulsa is better known as an industry town than a vacation spot. But it's precisely the steady wealth from its oil fields and refineries that has helped Tulsa become such a vibrant city – an unlikely tourist destination in the heartland of the US, with a unique blend of Oklahoma charm and cosmopolitan energy.

Tulsa's downtown has one of the most extensive assemblages of art deco architecture in the country. The lavishly detailed buildings so dominated the skyline in the 1920s and '30s that it was nicknamed the Terra-Cotta City for the building material used to create the distinctive detailing. Today, those same buildings are not only the subject of popular urban tours, they also help frame Tulsa's rich cultural scene, from trendy restaurants and street art to world-class museums, theaters and iconic music venues. Beyond downtown, Tulsa's green spaces also offer ample opportunities for outdoor recreation and community events.

GO IF YOU LIKE...
- *art deco architecture*
- *museums*
- *live music*
- *Black history*
- *music history*
- *the Midwest*

Why go to Tulsa?

Though Tulsa is best known for its oil riches and art deco architecture, it makes for a surprisingly engaging destination for museum-lovers. Well-funded and beloved art institutions like the Philbrook and Gilcrease museums have been welcoming visitors since the 1940s. Newer additions are no less compelling: the Greenwood Rising museum examines the horrific 1921 race-based attack on the city's 'Black Wall Street,' while the work and legacy of two American folk music legends can be found at the Woody Guthrie Center and Bob Dylan Museum. Tulsa's public spaces, too, have expanded to include the Gathering Place, an artsy park and community space, as well as restored sections of the famous Route 66. Add to that a revitalized downtown and a thriving music scene with a friendly Midwestern vibe, and the appeal of Tulsa is as undeniable as it is unexpected.

GETTING THERE

Tulsa International Airport is the city's main gateway, with nonstop flights from several US destinations. It's located just eight miles northeast of downtown, making it quick to access. Driving or taking a long-distance bus is easy, though the closest big cities, Dallas and Kansas City, are both about four hours away. Tulsa is located just off I-44 and north of I-40.

WHEN TO GO

Sep – Nov

Autumn in Tulsa provides a window of temperate weather, making it an optimal time to visit: the spring tornado season has passed, the heat of the summer is over and winter's frigid temperatures have not set in.

FIRST-TIME TIPS

Check out *TulsaPeople* (tulsapeople.com) for goings-on around town, including the city's lively music scene.

....

For a deep dive into Tulsa's historic neighborhoods, book a customized walking tour with *Tours of Tulsa* (toursoftulsa.com).

....

Tulsa's public bus system is *incredibly limited* so don't bank on using it. Instead, walk and use a bikeshare (thismachinetulsa.com) or e-scooter. For places further afield – or if you simply prefer four wheels – take a rideshare like Uber and Lyft.

....

Big chain hotels are the go-to in Tulsa, but for something less cookie-cutter, stay in a *retro motel* on East 11th St.

Opposite: Manicured gardens at the Philbrook Museum of Art. **Above, left**: The riverfront Gathering Place park; **right**: retro gas station on Route 66

AMAZING CROWD-FREE EXPERIENCES

 Stroll through the Deco District in downtown Tulsa, where art deco architecture, vibrant murals, trendy boutiques and tony restaurants abound.

 Learn about the lives and timeless tunes of the namesake folk legends at the Woody Guthrie Center and Bob Dylan Center in the Arts District.

 Tour the historic Greenwood District to learn about the 1921 Tulsa Race Massacre, with must-see stops at the Greenwood Rising museum and John Hope Franklin Reconciliation Park.

 Go to a concert at the historic Cain's Ballroom, a one-time car garage turned iconic venue for top musicians, from big band to punk.

 Visit the Gilcrease Museum (undergoing renovations at press time), with one of the most comprehensive collections of art from the American West, from the colonial era to the modern day.

 Enjoy the mind-bending playgrounds and large-scale art at the Gathering Place, an expansive riverfront park with trails, community events and a hands-on STEM museum.

Opposite: Bluebonnets blooming in Hill Country

Texas Hill Country Texas

WINE TASTING, BARBEQUE AND CAMPING AMONG THE WILDFLOWERS

OKLAHOMA

NEW MEXICO

TEXAS

Texas Hill Country

MEXICO

old country. The best way to visit is on a road trip; explore the attractive highways that connect these settlements, stopping along the way to sample local wines or hike and paddle through the many state parks.

Climb to the top of the pink granite dome at the center of Enchanted Rock State Natural Area or descend into the caves of Kickapoo Cavern or Longhorn Cavern State Parks. As the temperature rises – and in central Texas you can be sure that it will – plunge into Pedernales Falls or join locals tubing on the Guadalupe River outside of New Braunfels.

GO IF YOU LIKE...
- ♥ *Napa Valley*
- ♥ *slow-cooked BBQ*
- ♥ *wildflowers*
- ♥ *small-town charm*
- ♥ *backroads*
- ♥ *romantic B&Bs*

Picture this: you're driving along backcountry highways, with the occasional stop at rural wineries before overnighting at a small B&B with sweeping vineyard views. No, you're not in Napa Valley, but Texas Hill Country.

Waves of Czech and German immigrants founded towns such as Fredericksburg and Boerne here in the late 1800s, bringing with them a penchant for cute churches and planting grapes and hops from the

Why go to Texas Hill Country?

While Texas stereotypes center on cowboys galloping across the windblown desert, the state's true topographical diversity is at its best in the Hill Country. The rolling hills west of Austin and San Antonio are covered with oak forests and watered by natural springs and the Colorado River, itself a popular destination for swimming and paddling.

Hill Country is home to at least one hundred wineries, of which 60 are clustered around the town of Fredericksburg. The latter is a popular base for spending the day bouncing between tastings, with perhaps a lunch stop for famous Texas barbecue en route.

Active visitors opt instead for the fifteen state parks and natural areas spread across the Hill Country. Popular destinations like Enchanted Rock and Hamilton Pool do see crowds, and you'll want to reserve in advance if you hope to snag a campsite, but further-flung areas are typically quiet.

GETTING THERE

Austin-Bergstrom International Airport is a mini-hub for American and Southwest Airlines, and connects the city to destinations across the US, Europe and Central America. Austin is also a stop on Amtrak's *Texas Eagle* train route, which runs between Chicago and Los Angeles. Fredericksburg is 1½ hours west of Austin by car.

WHEN TO GO

Mar – May

Blooming Texas bluebonnets showcase the best of the state's wildflowers, while sunny days are still cool enough to explore the many state parks and natural areas.

FIRST-TIME TIPS

Austinites head to the Hill Country en masse on weekends, so try to time your visit for quieter weekdays if possible.

....

Most barbecue joints in Central Texas are community affairs – order by weight for meat and sides, then belly up to a long shared table wherever there's space.

....

The 13-mile Willow City Loop outside Fredericksburg is wildflower central during peak season, but expect to join crowds of locals searching for an iconic bluebonnet portrait.

....

If nobody wants to be the designated driver, Fredericksburg's 290 Wine Shuttle runs frequently between the town and surrounding wineries on weekends.

Left: Oak-shaded picnic tables in Texas wine country. **Opposite, left**: Pedernales Falls; **right**: Kickapoo Cavern's limestone marvels

AMAZING CROWD-FREE EXPERIENCES

 Head to Balcones Canyonlands National Wildlife Refuge for crowd- and fee-free hiking trails. Or try the less-visited state parks at Lost Maples and Colorado Bend.

 Get away from the Guadalupe River party scene while kayaking under the cypress trees overhanging the Medina River.

 Follow in the footsteps of a Texas legend at Lyndon B Johnson National Historical Park and nearby LBJ Ranch, where the former president grew up.

 Avoid the crowds of Austin's bat bridge and watch the twilight flight of 3 million Mexican free-tailed bats out of Fredericksburg's Old Tunnel.

 Sing along with country music classics in little Lukenbach's dance hall, made famous by artist Waylon Jennings. It's an unforgettable way to while away a Texas afternoon.

 Embrace your inner cowboy on a dude ranch horse ride; there's a cluster around Bandera, which calls itself the 'Cowboy Capital of Texas.'

Rio Grande Valley Texas

UNBEATABLE BIRD-WATCHING AND TEX-MEX CUISINE IN SOUTHERN TEXAS

the other side of the Rio Grande River, while migratory birds soar through the skies above, transitioning between tropical climates of Mexico and subtropical south Texas. Another sort of migratory breed, the winter Texan, flocks here each year to escape the cold further north and enjoy the incredible cuisine and intercultural heritage that defines the Rio Grande Valley.

History buffs poke around the restored downtowns that played important roles in the political events leading up to the Mexican–American and Civil Wars, which defined the borders of modern Texas as we know them today.

GO IF YOU LIKE...

- *fusion cuisine*
- *bird-watching*
- *Florida winters*
- *frontier history*
- *South Padre Island*
- *monarch butterflies*

Skip the massive crowds of South Padre Island's beaches – where visitors number over 2 million during Spring Break – and opt instead for the extensive network of state parks and bird-watching sites that extend up the lower Rio Grande Valley of southern Texas.

This region hugging the US–Mexico border blends the two cultures into something unique, for which the locals are rightly proud. Residents hop back and forth to Mexico for weekend shopping trips or to visit family on

Why go to the Rio Grande Valley?

Dining in the Rio Grande Valley is reason enough to visit. Your stomach will thank you the entire way, from the taco stands in Laredo down to Texas' last pit-smoked barbacoa at Vera's Backyard in Brownsville – and don't forget about local chains like Delia's Tamales and Taco Palenque. Historic old town centers still carry the history of the pre-Texas Rio Grande Valley, both as a Mexican state and as the independent Republic of the Rio Grande.

Beyond the cities, the World Birding Center unites nine distinct ecotourism sites along the lower Rio Grande, combining diverse habitats like the shallow marsh wetlands at Estero Llano Grande and oxbow lakes of Resaca de la Palma with the mesquite woods of Hidalgo's Old Pumphouse. Managed by a variety of state and national authorities, all nine sites are open to the public. Expect visits from over five hundred bird species, which keeps the birders coming back year after year.

GETTING THERE

Small airports in McAllen, Laredo and Brownsville are served by flights to international hubs in Houston and Dallas, with additional service between McAllen and Las Vegas. All three cities are also served by regional bus services and international routes crossing the border into Mexico.

WHEN TO GO

Feb – May

Early spring sees pleasant weather for hiking in the Rio Grande floodplain and the Charro Days cultural festival in Brownsville, while April and May is peak bird-watching time during the spring migration.

AMAZING CROWD-FREE EXPERIENCES

 Meet the sunrise at Bentsen–Rio Grande Valley State Park's Hawk Observation Tower, perfect for bird-watching from above the forest canopy.

 Stretch out on the sands at undeveloped Boca Chica State Park's 1055 acres of coastal dunes. They're mostly empty, though occasionally closed for SpaceX launches.

 Ride the hand-pulled Los Ebanos Ferry, the last of its kind on the US–Mexico border. It crosses from McAllen to the town of Gustavo Díaz Ordaz.

 Keep an eye out for the Tamaulipas crow, a species whose known range extends just across the border into the Brownsville landfill, making it an unexpected bird-watching hotspot.

 Follow the flow of the first battle of the Mexican-American War with the engaging staff and on-site signage at Palo Alto Battlefield Historic Site in Brownsville.

 Camp overnight at Falcon State Park, prime bird-watching and butterfly migration territory alongside the 28-mile Falcon International Reservoir.

Opposite, top: Charro Days fiesta in Brownsville; **bottom**: Starbase spaceport in Boca Chica

FIRST-TIME TIPS

In this <u>multicultural border community</u> Spanish is just as prevalent as English, so brush up on the basics before your arrival.

Closures of Boca Chica for SpaceX Starship launch activities are a common point of contention for RGV locals – appeals are still pending over a lawsuit that claims it violates the state constitution. <u>Check locally</u> whether Hwy 4 to Boca Chica and the adjacent Lower Rio Grande National Wildlife Refuge is open before setting out from Brownsville.

Expect lines at <u>Customs and Border Patrol checkpoints</u> on the way out of south Texas. Officers will verify the citizenship of all travelers in a vehicle and may conduct further searches.

This spread:
Garden of the Gods, Illinois

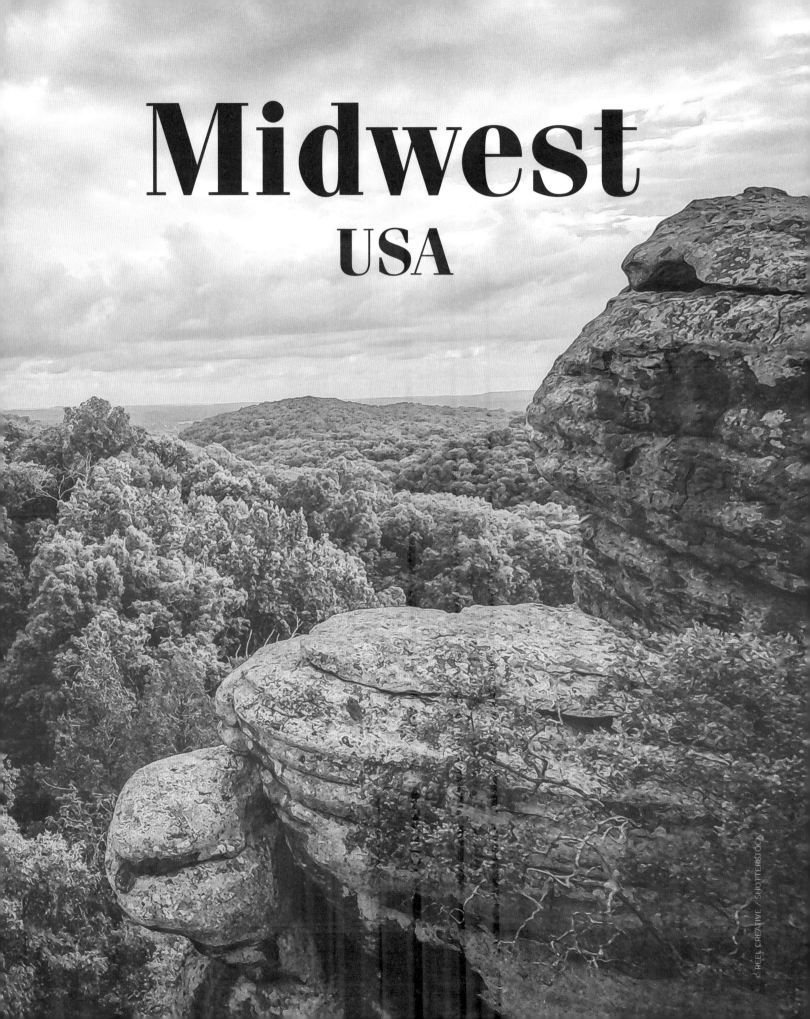

Midwest
USA

North Dakota Badlands North Dakota

SCENIC SOLITUDE IN THE SHADOW OF THEODORE ROOSEVELT NATIONAL PARK

CANADA

NEW MEXICO

NORTH DAKOTA

North Dakota
Badlands

MINNESOTA

SOUTH DAKOTA

The fresh scent of sweet clover rises up along the ridgeline. Juniper, yucca and thirsty cottonwoods stand out as smudges of green against the craggy bluffs and wind-chiseled canyons, striped in charcoal and khaki, brick and bone. This is North Dakota's western edge, where the prairie meets the sunbaked badlands.

President Roosevelt once operated a ranch here, on land that's now the national park that bears his name, and his legacy still resonates. The park's three units are connected by the 144-mile Maah Daah Hey Trail (among the most startlingly scenic singletrack routes in the country), the glinting waters of the Little Missouri River and the Little Missouri National Grassland – the largest in the United States.

A remote location and North Dakota's small population means Theodore Roosevelt National Park (TRNP) only sees an average of 668,000 visitors per year. That's nothing compared to the nearest national parks, including South Dakota's Badlands (1 million), Glacier (2.9 million) and Yellowstone (3.3 million). Out here, you'll likely see more bison and chattering prairie dogs than people.

GO IF YOU LIKE...
- 🤍 *wildlife watching*
- 🤍 *hiking and cycling*
- 🤍 *Old West history*
- 🤍 *quirky towns*
- 🤍 *cowboy culture*

Why go to the North Dakota Badlands?

Medora, a tiny town near the park's South Unit, offers a taste of socialization with mom-and-pop shops, restaurants and family-friendly entertainment. Nearby lodging includes campgrounds, rustic shepherd's wagons and an upscale Old West-style hotel.

Classic Medora flavors include rich bison osso buco from Theodore's Dining Room, cowboy-style BBQ at the Pitchfork Steak Fondue and Juneberry ice cream. Expanded grab-and-go options from Badlands Pizza and Bread + Butter serve picnickers, while lighter fare from the Farmhouse Café and Medora Uncork'd counters hearty cattle-country entrees.

The new Point to Point Park provides a much-needed pool, lazy river and free splash pad to beat the heat. Zoom over Medora on the Manitou Zipline or climb the butte for a challenging hike and an excellent view. Half of the reimagined 18-hole mini-golf course is built right into the bluff. The highly anticipated Theodore Roosevelt National Library will open in 2026.

Below, left: Mountain biking the Maah Daah Hey trail; **right**: mustangs in a sunset meadow. **Opposite**: Theodore Roosevelt's log cabin

GETTING THERE

The park's North and South Units are 70 miles apart, so most visitors come by car, camper or RV – or they fly in and rent a car at the airport. The closest international airport is in Minot, a three-hour drive from Medora and about 2½ hours from the North Unit. Flights to Dickinson or Bismarck decrease drive time.

WHEN TO GO

May – Sep

Every Medora attraction is open mid-June through early September, during the *Medora Musical* run, but visits to Theodore Roosevelt National Park only top 100,000 a month in June, July and August. Even then, the park's three units don't feel crowded.

FIRST-TIME TIPS

The badlands can be hot and arid, so avoid midday hikes in summer and pack plenty of water.

Stock up on snacks in Dickinson or Watford City – there isn't a grocery store in Medora.

Many trails cross grazing land, so close the cattle gates along the way to keep the cows out.

Stay at least 25 yards away from wildlife, especially bison, which can run 35 miles per hour.

Only road cycling is allowed in Theodore Roosevelt National Park. Use Buffalo Gap Trail to bypass the South Unit and rejoin the Maah Daah Hey Trail.

AMAZING CROWD-FREE EXPERIENCES

 Cruise the scenic byways, passing prairie dog towns and sunset views in TRNP's South Unit and soaring Little Missouri River overlooks in the North.

 Hike down into Painted Canyon, through a petrified forest, then climb Buck Hill, the park's highest accessible point. Skyline Vista and the Little Mo Nature Trail inner loop are paved.

 Watch wildlife, including elk and wild horses in the South Unit, longhorn cattle and golden eagles in the North, and bison and deer throughout.

 Tackle the Maah Daah Hey Trail. Dakota Cyclery provides bike rentals and shuttle service. CCC Campground, Cottonwood Campground and Elkhorn Camp are near (or inside) TRNP.

 Shop for Pendleton blankets, jewelry and cowboy boots in Medora. Original works from Western Edge Books, Art and Music have a distinct frontier flavor.

 Dive into history at The Teddy Roosevelt Show, chat with a Roosevelt reenactor, then visit the Cowboy Hall of Fame and Roosevelt's Elkhorn Ranch.

Downtown Fargo North Dakota

CULTURE, CUISINE AND COMMUNITY IN A NORTH DAKOTA NEIGHBORHOOD

CANADA

NEW MEXICO

NORTH DAKOTA

Fargo

MINNESOTA

SOUTH DAKOTA

Don't forget the spray paint when you come to Fargo's Art Alley – a place where anyone can make their mark. This ever-evolving community art project is just one of many gathering places in the walkable downtown.

Fargo's scrappy DIY spirit is fueled by a collaborative art, food and beer scene, a steady stream of college students, a tradition of entrepreneurship and enterprising immigrants from Africa, Asia, Europe, North America and the Middle East. Chat with culture bearers at the Indigenous Art Fair, meet home cooks at Fargo-Moorhead International Potluck and create something new during classes, community art projects and street festivals all year long.

Farmland surrounds North Dakota's largest city, so the region's meat, honey, grains and produce pop up on menus and in markets. Sip experimental cider at Wild Terra, pair buffalo sausage with a Fargo brew at Wurst Bier Hall or nibble béchamel-topped pizza made with North Dakota flour at Blackbird Woodfire.

GO IF YOU LIKE...
- *city strolls*
- *public art*
- *diverse dining*
- *street festivals*
- *craft beverages*
- *local shops*

Why go to downtown Fargo?

Creativity, commerce and community collide downtown. Jasper Hotel, the city's newest boutique property, hosts local art exhibits, film screenings and a jazz brunch inside its farm-to-table restaurant. Hotel Donaldson renovations expanded the rooftop patio and updated 17 suites that showcase regional art. (It's like sleeping in a gallery, just with turndown service.)

Come to Parachigo art studio and DIY space for live music, a community kiln, craft swaps, flash tattoos and a dry bar. Stop by the 1889 for cooking, crafting and pottery classes that spill out of one of the oldest buildings in the city. Find gifts, clothing and food from more than 18 local artists, farmers, ranchers and entrepreneurs at First Avenue Market, a new shop with an old school vibe.

A $66 million building project moves the Fargo Moorhead Community Theatre, a fixture since 1946, into the neighborhood. The next generation of performers will step on stage downtown.

GETTING THERE

Fly direct to Fargo's Hector International Airport from 10 states. Buses stop downtown (Greyhound) and 12 blocks north of the city center (Jefferson Lines). Landline also shuttles travelers between the Fargo and Minneapolis–St Paul airports. Amtrak's *Empire Builder* (which links Chicago and the Pacific Northwest) arrives and departs from the downtown station well after midnight. Taxis, rideshares and car rentals are available.

WHEN TO GO

Apr – Nov

Fargoans play outside all winter, but visitors prefer the city's sunny spring weather, long summer days and brisk fall nights. Most street festivals fall between July and early November, but the neighborhood is lively all year long.

AMAZING CROWD-FREE EXPERIENCES

 Spot public art, including murals, sculptures and boxcars. Plains Art Museum (which emphasizes modern art and Indigenous works) is also free.

 Taste the world. Try bubble tea, bibimbap, tamales, Thai ice cream, French pastries, Nepali momos, plantains, dolma and knishes at intimate eateries and food trucks.

 Hear bands in an ex-church (Sanctuary Events Center), an Irish pub (Dempsey's Public House), the kitschy Troll Lounge or the Hall at Fargo Brewing Company's indoor and outdoor stages.

 Picnic and play (or swim!) in shady Island Park. Find movies, ice skating, live music, dance classes and a splash pad at Broadway Square.

 Attend a festival. Red River Market, Downtown Fargo Street Fair and the Island Park Show are summer favorites. Bundle up for November's holiday parade and Christmas market.

 Buy books at Zandbroz Variety, eclectic decor at O'Day Cache, a plethora of plants at Botanical Brothers, plus vintage shops, record stores and clothing boutiques in between.

FIRST-TIME TIPS

So many visitors listed North Dakota as <u>their 50th state</u> that tourism officials just went with it. Score a 'Best for Last' T-shirt at Gallery 4, the state's oldest co-op gallery.

....

Cross the Red River of the North to step into Minnesota. The <u>Hjemkomst Center</u> details regional history and rents kayaks, snowshoes and cross-country skis for exploring the riverside park.

....

<u>Parking on downtown ramps is free</u> on evenings and weekends.

....

<u>Bikes are allowed on sidewalks</u> everywhere except along Broadway between NP Avenue and 6th Avenue North.

....

Some shops are <u>closed on Sundays</u>.

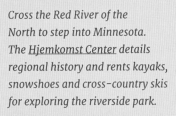

Above: Art Alley is splashed with graffiti; **left**: downtown is better with a hot dog in hand

157

Opposite: A mountain
with profound spiritual
significance

Bear Butte South Dakota

A SACRED MOUNTAIN FOR GENERATIONS OF NATIVE AMERICANS

layers millions of years ago, is an important sacred site for many Native American tribes.

The Lakota Sioux call it *Mato Paha* or Bear Mountain. For centuries they have come here for spiritual inspiration, steeping the mountain in countless prayers. On the public trail to the top are many reminders that this is holy ground. Almost every tree and bush is draped with colorful prayer flags and strung with tiny bundles of tobacco.

It's a rigorous 3-mile round-trip hike to the 4426-foot Bear Butte summit, but it has an indefinable quality that elicits a sense of wonder.

Crossing the South Dakota plains from the east, you'll see the granite domes and dark pine forests of the Black Hills gradually materialize on the horizon. Standing apart is a worn and ancient mountain, rising over the prairie as if guarding the approach. Among the many scenic attractions in the Black Hills, Bear Butte doesn't take top billing, but for many here, it's of enormous spiritual importance. This mass of igneous rock, which pushed up through sedimentary

GO IF YOU LIKE...
- 💜 *Native American history*
- 💜 *sacred sites*
- 💜 *wildlife spotting*
- 💜 *hiking*
- 💜 *the Black Hills*
- 💜 *fishing*

159

Why go to Bear Butte?

'This mountain is a dynamic and living cathedral. It is a Sacred Place. We are all visitors at this special place.' So reads the sign at the entrance to Bear Butte State Park. Native Americans say that spiritual awakenings can and will occur on the hike up to the summit. As you climb the trail, passing small clusters of tough ponderosa pine and juniper trees, you may even hear the sound of ceremonial drums – a faint heartbeat that seems to resonate from deep within the rocks.

To cap off this ethereal experience, spend the night at one of the campsites nestled near the base of the mountain, watching the sunlight fade into star-pricked darkness. And when you wake, take advantage of the other activities nearby. Go boating at Bear Butte Lake, fish off the pier and wave at the local herd of bison. Or why not climb the butte one last time?

GETTING THERE

Bear Butte State Park is located just 15 minutes northeast of the town of Sturgis, off Hwy 79. The nearest major airport is Rapid City, which is an hour's drive away. You'll need your own wheels.

WHEN TO GO

May – Oct

Summer vacation (Jun–Aug) is high season, so you may see something that vaguely resembles a crowd. The Sturgis Motorcycle Rally takes place in early August, attracting half a million bikers annually.

Bottom, left: Granite spires in Custer State Park; **right**: offerings and prayer flags at Bear Butte. **Opposite**: Lakota chief Red Cloud made a pilgrimage to Bear Butte

FIRST-TIME TIPS

Visit the Educational Center, open May until September, which highlights the mountain's geology, history and the cultural beliefs of the Northern Plains Indians.

As a sacred site for over 30 Native American tribes, Bear Butte often hosts prayer ceremonies. Visitors should be respectful and refrain from taking photographs.

There are 15 campsites located in Bear Butte State Park, but they do not take reservations. It's first come, first served only.

If you visit in September, be sure to hit the nearby Custer State Park Buffalo Roundup. Around 1300 bison are herded into corrals during this spectacular event.

AMAZING CROWD-FREE EXPERIENCES

 Take the Lake Trail (the other hiking trail in the park), which is just over 2 miles long and circles Bear Butte Lake. You probably won't see another soul.

 Lace up your hiking boots and head out on the northernmost section of the 111-mile Centennial Trail, which traverses the park.

 Keep an eagle eye out for local wildlife, including deer, bison, porcupines and rattlesnakes. Bird-watching might snare you a mountain bluebird, northern flicker woodpecker or spotted towhee.

 Get lost amid the granite spires and domes of the 71,000-acre Custer State Park, less than one hour away.

 Reminisce about hogs of old at the nearby Sturgis Motorcycle Museum, which showcases unique and historic motorcycles that date back to 1905.

 Cast a line into Bear Butte Lake to catch northern pike, white crappie, yellow bullhead and yellow perch.

The Iron Range Minnesota

HISTORY MEETS SCUBA DIVING IN AN UNHERALDED CORNER OF MINNESOTA

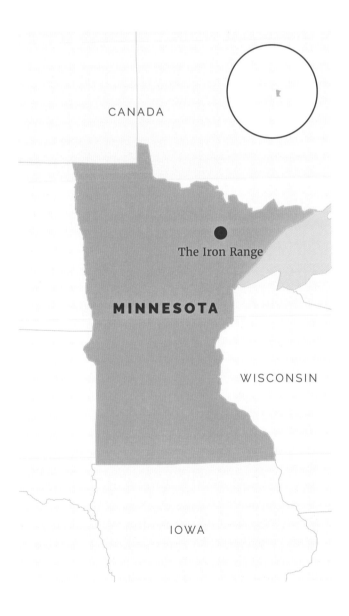

CANADA

The Iron Range

MINNESOTA

WISCONSIN

IOWA

Stretching 175 miles from southwest to northeast Minnesota, the Iron Range is often overlooked but rarely unappreciated. Six active mines are located in the densely forested region and lend a rich backstory with stunning natural beauty to match. There are three distinct iron-ore districts: Cuyuna in the south, Mesabi in the center and Vermillion in the northeast. Ask any Minnesotan and they'll likely have a preference for one range over another – with a detailed explanation as to why – though you'll find pristine nature everywhere you look.

Iron ore was first discovered in Minnesota in 1884 in the Vermillion Range, followed by finds in Mesabi in 1892 and Cuyuna in 1911. Decades of mining and development resulted in a population boom, comprised of immigrants from over 20 European countries. While you'll find plenty of activity here, it still feels like the middle of nowhere at its finest. Towns are few and far between, and more often than not flanked by glass-like lakes and dense woodlands.

GO IF YOU LIKE...
- *history*
- *hiking trails*
- *geology and mining*
- *cross-country skiing*
- *small towns*
- *scuba diving*

Why go to the Iron Range?

Minnesota has no shortage of lakes – 11,842 to be exact. And in the Iron Range, there's a good chance that you'll have one all to yourself. Further off the beaten path than its popular counterparts near the Twin Cities or Lake Superior, the region is a great place to get off the grid and unwind.

But if you like to stay busy, don't worry – there's plenty to do. Most people don't think of Minnesota as a scuba-diving location, but spring-fed Iron Range lakes, some of which are flooded pit mines, offer a unique twist on underwater exploration. Lake Ore-be-Gone in Gilbert, some four hundred feet deep, is home to a sunken plane wreck and plenty of walleye fish. Above ground, the Lost 40 Scientific and Natural Area is home to one of the state's only old-growth pine forests; many of the trees here are three to four hundred years old.

GETTING THERE

It feels like a world away from Minneapolis and St Paul, but the town of Crosby at the lower end of the Iron Range is only a two-hour drive from the Twin Cities. If traveling further north, count on a four-hour trip. Car rental is available at Minneapolis–St Paul International Airport.

WHEN TO GO

Jun – Aug

Believe it or not, you can visit year-round. Summer, however, is unbeatable. Temperatures hover in the upper 70s and sunshine is abundant.

AMAZING CROWD-FREE EXPERIENCES

Camp at Bear Head Lake State Park. Whether you're gliding along in a canoe or hiking the Beach Trail, wildlife abounds.

Visit Ely, the charming gateway to the Boundary Waters Canoe Area, where you can hike to the 70-foot Kawishiwi Falls or kick back for a bite to eat in town.

Hike or bike through Chippewa National Forest, a sprawling forest that is the homeland of the Dakota and Ojibwe peoples. There are nearly three hundred miles of trails.

Cycle or kayak at Redhead Mountain Bike Park. This formerly abandoned mine in Chisholm now has 25 miles of trails, exploring a network of lakes.

Visit the Minnesota Museum of Mining. Learn more about the Iron Range's historical background before heading out to see it in real life.

Admire the Oldtown-Finntown Overlook, a mining canyon encircled by sheer rust-colored cliffs.

Above: Minnesota's calm lakes are ideal for canoeing; below: pristine waters at Bear Head State Park

Opposite: The treetops look painted red and orange in autumn

Superior National Forest Minnesota

TAKE TO THE WATER IN MINNESOTA'S SECLUDED NORTHEAST

V ast woodlands and bountiful waterways mingle within Superior National Forest, a treasured landscape sprawling across 3.9 million acres in the northeastern corner of Minnesota. Once navigated by Indigenous communities and loggers, the forest is rich in cultural history and lore. What differentiates Superior National Forest from the rest of the state is the sheer amount of water – the lakes and rivers here cover more than 445,000 acres.

The cherished Boundary Waters Canoe Area (BWCA), an impressive and remote network of waterways on the border of the US and Canada, makes up roughly one-third of Superior National Forest. For paddlers, it's a dream destination with over 1500 miles of canoe routes, but even those who aren't water savvy will appreciate the rugged beauty of the landscape.

As the name suggests, Superior National Forest also borders the vast Lake Superior, where you'll find plenty of bird's-eye views from rocky bluffs and lighthouses. If anything, the only difficulty you'll face is trying to choose which bodies of water you want to visit.

GO IF YOU LIKE...
- 💜 *secluded wilderness*
- 💜 *canoeing*
- 💜 *adventurous travel*
- 💜 *bird-watching*
- 💜 *camping*

167

Why go to Superior National Forest?

Superior National Forest and the Boundary Waters may get a lot of hype, but they are worth every ounce. And while they're a popular destination for Minnesotans and Midwesterners, the woodlands and lakes remain deeply secluded. For the most part, they're untouched by human activity, apart from the occasional canoe.

Among the pine and spruce trees, wildlife thrives. Deer, moose, bears and even wolves – plus over 250 species of birds – make Superior National Forest an unrivaled place for viewing Minnesota's native species. For the most immersive experience, be sure to camp out. With over two thousand campsites to choose from, you're spoiled for choice in one of the country's most pristine natural areas. And if sleeping in a tent sounds like a little bit too much adventure, fret not: there are a wide range of accommodation options closer to civilization.

GETTING THERE

Regardless of your ultimate destination, expect to drive around three or four hours from the Twin Cities. The southern part of the forest is near Silver Bay, just over three hours north of the Minneapolis–St Paul International Airport. To reach the Boundary Waters Canoe Area near Ely, you're looking at a four-hour drive.

WHEN TO GO

Jun – Oct

Enthusiastic Minnesotans would say each season has its own appeal, but the best time to visit is arguably in summer or fall, when it's either warm and sunny or crisp and awash in autumn colors.

AMAZING CROWD-FREE EXPERIENCES

 Canoe around the Boundary Waters Canoe Area (BWCA). There are plenty of outfitters in Ely, where it's easy to grab a boat rental and spend a day or more on the water.

 Go fishing for walleye, trout, bass and more. Take your pick with 695 sq miles of surface water in Superior National Forest.

 Trek around the Lutsen Mountains, where people ski in winter and hike through flower-filled meadows in summer.

 Check out Split Rock Lighthouse. This lighthouse stands high on the edge of a jagged cliff overlooking Lake Superior.

 Experience small town Minnesota charm in Grand Marais, way up on the North Shore of Lake Superior.

 Hike Eagle Mountain Trail, a 3.5-mile trail leading to the highest natural point in Minnesota. Don't forget a permit – you'll need one for all travel within the BWCA, whether canoeing or hiking.

Clockwise from top: Finding solitude at a lakeside campground; historic Split Rock Lighthouse; Superior is the largest national forest east of the Mississippi

Ice Age Trail Wisconsin

HIKE THROUGH GLACIER-CARVED LANDSCAPES ON THIS LONG-DISTANCE TREK

MICHIGAN

MINNESOTA

WISCONSIN

Ice Age Trail

yellow-blazed Ice Age segments and the rest along connecting paths and country roads. So get bragging rights while you can. The grand backpacking experience combines DIY camping with trail towns to refresh in with food and lodging. For hikers intimidated by the Appalachian or Pacific Crest Trails, the Ice Age Trail offers a shorter, less strenuous alternative.

Plus, you'll boost your glacial geology knowledge. Moraines (ridges), kettles (crater-like depressions) and kames (conical hills) pop up along the way, features not found on other long-distance paths.

GO IF YOU LIKE...
- *the Appalachian Trail*
- *backwoods camping*
- *small towns*
- *fall colors*
- *glacial remnants*
- *wildflowers*

Back when wooly mammoths and saber-toothed cats roamed the earth, a great glacier covered much of the north country. The Ice Age Trail follows that glacier's edge and takes in the wooded hills and glittering lakes it left behind. The route zigzags across Wisconsin for 1200 miles, passing through dense forests and flower-carpeted valleys, over stream crossings and up steep ridges with views across the horizon. Only around four hundred people have hiked it in its entirety, perhaps because it's still a work in progress, with some six hundred miles along

Why travel the Ice Age Trail?

The Ice Age Trail remains remarkably noncommodified, with few hikers and little media attention focused on its untrammeled course through Wisconsin's woods and lake lands. The route passes through many small communities, which is by design – it helps to connect travelers with locals. Opportunities abound to join them in building boardwalks, clearing brush, marking blazes and other activities. That's right: you can also be a true trailblazer on the Ice Age Trail. New segments like White Cedar (through a cedar swamp) and Rib Lake (along ridges and streams) add to the path each year, and new trail communities like Portage and Baraboo welcome hikers with fresh eating and snoozing options. A network of dedicated volunteers helps make life easy for hikers, providing information on everything from bear sightings and day-hike options to which farmers let you pitch a tent on their property.

GETTING THERE

The trail's western end is in Interstate State Park in St Croix Falls, Minnesota, about 55 miles from Minneapolis, a plane, train and bus hub. The trail's eastern end is in Potawatomi State Park in Sturgeon Bay, Wisconsin. It's trickier to reach, with Milwaukee being the nearest hub 160 miles away. From either spot you'll need wheels to reach the trailheads.

WHEN TO GO

Apr – Oct

April and May offer moderate temperatures and wildflowers. June through August brings lots of daylight, but annoying insects. September and October burst with fall foliage. Winter is the least busy time, with cold and snow.

FIRST-TIME TIPS

The Ice Age Trail Guidebook, atlas and app are essential resources; purchase them through the Ice Age Trail Alliance (iceagetrail. org).

The Ice Age Trail is <u>blazed</u> in yellow, side trails are blazed white and connector routes are blazed blue.

Volunteer trail angels provide assistance in the form of <u>shuttles, lodging, showers and more</u>. The Trail Alliance has contact information.

Some parts of the trail <u>close in winter</u> during various hunting seasons.

Pack hiking boots, rain gear, a tent and sleeping bag. <u>Resupply</u> at grocery stores in towns en route.

AMAZING CROWD-FREE EXPERIENCES

 Take a break in a trail community and chat with locals over bratwursts, cheese curds, ice cream and beer.

 Pitch a tent under the stars. The trail has 23 designated primitive camping areas where it'll just be you and the odd wolf howl.

 Forest bathe on the Lake Eleven or Mondeaux Esker segments, some of the trail's most remote sections that veer deep into the rugged Northwoods.

 Day hike to Blue Spring Lake, Scuppernong or other easy spots in Kettle Moraine State Forest's southern unit, where icy springs, pinewoods and bluff-top views await.

 Feel the glaciers' power on the Chippewa Moraine segment, which goes up hills, down valleys and around 20 kettle lakes cut by ancient ice sheets.

 Meander over stone bridges, waterfalls and rock formations on the river-hugging Dells of the Eau Claire segment.

Above: Geological features add drama to the views in Devil's Lake State Park

Opposite: The Fenelon Place Elevator offers a short but sweet joyride

Dubuque Iowa

WHERE IOWA STARTED, AND WHERE IOWA'S HEADED

MINNESOTA

IOWA

Dubuque

ILLINOIS

MISSOURI

In the Millwork District, a new crop of independent boutiques, restaurants serving local produce and microbreweries has sprung up. One of the best is Backpocket Brewing (HQ is in Coralville, 90 miles southwest). The taproom also has a 'beercade,' packed with retro arcade games and duckpin bowling.

The art scene is buzzing, too. One creative local project, 'Voices Productions,' started as an art gallery in the Millwork District but has since exploded onto the streets of the city in the form of over 45 colorful murals. Created by local artists and the graduates of the mural workshops, the artwork encourages people to explore the city – and it's working.

Leave clichés about cornfields at the door: east Iowa is undergoing a renaissance and Dubuque is leading the way. The homelands of the fur-trading Meskwaki, Dubuque was where the first Europeans settled in Iowa – notably, the lead miner Julien Dubuque, who founded his namesake town in the late 1700s. Though it's Iowa's oldest city, Dubuque is on the rise again.

GO IF YOU LIKE...
- *St Louis*
- *river cruising*
- *nature*
- *microbreweries*
- *baseball*
- *local art*

Why go to Dubuque?

Just west of the Mississippi River, bordering Illinois and Wisconsin on the eastern side and only three hours from state capital Des Moines, Dubuque is well-situated for outside visitors. Tourist numbers are on the rise, and it's no wonder: beyond downtown Dubuque's revitalized art scene, the town is also a great base to experience east Iowa's caves, river cruises and historic attractions.

And let's not forget the classic 1989 movie *Field of Dreams*, which was filmed at a farm just outside of Dyersville in Dubuque County. The movie location is open to the public for free, so you can unleash your inner Kevin Costner, play a game on the baseball diamond in front of the farm house or re-create movie scenes when ghost players emerge from the cornfield. Visit the 'If You Build It' exhibition in downtown Dyersville to experience the history of the movie in full.

GETTING THERE

Dubuque is a port of call for several Mississippi River cruises. One of the largest is Viking, which operates cruises from St Louis to St Paul with a stop in Dubuque. The nearest major airport is Chicago O'Hare, approximately three hours away from Dubuque by car.

WHEN TO GO

mid-Jul – Sep

Summer is the best time to visit. The weather is warm, river water levels are lower (perfect for boating and swimming) and there's a full calendar of events, such as the six-day Dubuque County Fair at the end of July.

FIRST-TIME TIPS

Mosquito season is from May to September; take precautions, especially if you're visiting spots along the Mississippi River. Avoid mayfly season, which usually occurs early July.

It's best to get around by car. East Iowa doesn't have much of a public transport system.

Check the weather. The state experiences climatic extremes, from tornados in May and June to cold, snowy winters.

Book a stay at the historic Hotel Julien Dubuque. It's said that gangster Al Capone used to stay there when he needed to escape from Chicago.

AMAZING CROWD-FREE EXPERIENCES

 Hike to the Julien Dubuque Monument at the Mines of Spain Recreation Area. This small castle-like structure overlooks the Mississippi.

 Watch the free 'Ghost Sundays' comedy show at the *Field of Dreams* movie site in Dyersville on Sundays in July and August. The ghosts of the Chicago White Sox have been entertaining crowds here for more than 30 years.

 Joyride the Fenelon Place Elevator. Dating back to 1882, it's the shortest and steepest funicular railway in the world.

 Cruise the Mississippi on the *Riverboat Twilight*, an elegant replica of a Victorian steamboat, with food, live entertainment and historical narration.

 In winter, head to Sundown Mountain for skiing and snowboarding. Visit Tuesdays to Thursdays for discounted lift passes and quieter slopes.

 Explore 16 caves and six miles of hiking trails at Maquoketa Caves State Park. Around 50% of the caves are walk-through; others involve a bit of crawling.

Opposite, left: Botanist Ada Hayden peeps out from a mural; **right**: the stocky Julien Dubuque monument overlooks the Mississippi River. **Above**: Reenacting scenes at the *Field of Dreams* movie location

The Flint Hills & West Kansas Kansas

FIND SOLITUDE AMONG ROLLING HILLS, OUTSIDER ART AND ALIEN ROCK FORMATIONS

COLORADO

KANSAS

The Flint Hills
& West Kansas

MISSOURI

Towering tallgrass and wildflowers waving in the wind, the horizon stretching as far as the eye can see with few signs of civilization: the iconic landscapes of the Flint Hills and western Kansas inevitably pull you back in time. This bison-dotted prairie once extended across over a third of the North American continent, but only those who drive along quiet country backroads can witness the small fragments of this magnificent ecosystem that remain today.

A town that's not even big enough to warrant a stoplight has one of the best small-town art scenes in the country, while huge chalky columns of limestone that are stuffed with ancient sea fossils – despite being nearly one thousand miles from the ocean – push up from the otherwise pancake-flat plains.

Many travelers zip by at 80mph, dismissing these regions as places to drive through, but the soft-spoken allure of America's heartland awaits those who make the stop.

GO IF YOU LIKE...
- ♥ *Theodore Roosevelt National Park*
- ♥ *Badlands National Park*
- ♥ *wide-open spaces*
- ♥ *folk art*
- ♥ *road trips*
- ♥ *offbeat outdoor adventures*

Why go to the Flint Hills and west Kansas?

Many miles from the mountains and the sea, rural Kansas doesn't have the kind of beauty that slaps you in the face, but instead one that slowly seeds itself in your soul. As our modern lives become more hustled, hassled and haggard, the timeless prairie and plains offer a soothing natural balm. Get in tune with the pace of the prairie during the summertime Symphony in the Flint Hills, which brings the scene to life with classical music and performances by local poets and storytellers.

Find more art and culture to the west in Lucas, a tiny town infused with an outsized personality. Grassroots and folk-art installations, many made by self-taught 'outsider' artists, decorate Lucas with a jolt of quirk, from Bowl Plaza, a mosaic-covered public bathroom shaped like a toilet covered in folk-art mosaics, to the world's largest collection of the world's smallest versions of the world's largest things (yes, really).

GETTING THERE

The best way to reach the Flint Hills and western Kansas is by car. Both I-70 and I-35 pass through or nearby. Small airports with extremely limited schedules (often just one or two flights per day) are located in Hays, Garden City and Salina. For more options, you'll have to start in Denver, Kansas City or Wichita.

WHEN TO GO

Apr – Jun, Sep & Oct

Spring and fall see the most pleasant weather, but be aware of spring and summer thunderstorms and tornadoes. The lack of shade and high humidity make being outside in summer a challenge, while blizzards can close parts of I-70 in winter.

FIRST-TIME TIPS

You have to hop off the not-so-interesting interstate to explore the best of these regions. Set aside enough time to <u>drive the charming backroads</u>, such as the 47-mile-long Flint Hills National Scenic Byway, which runs past the front gate of the Tallgrass Prairie National Preserve, and the Western Vistas Historic Byway near Little Jerusalem Badlands State Park, home to the state's limestone formations.

There's <u>precious little shade</u> in the treeless prairie, so make sure you've lathered on sunscreen and wear a hat before spending hours outdoors.

<u>Severe weather</u> rolls through the state frequently, so sign up for alerts on your phone.

AMAZING CROWD-FREE EXPERIENCES

 Trek to see the bison at Tallgrass Prairie National Preserve, once North America's largest continuous ecosystem.

 Dine on Kansas steak at Hays House, the oldest restaurant west of the Mississippi River, in Council Grove.

 Stop by Lucas to see the Garden of Eden. Civil War veteran SP Dinsmoor surrounded his house with strange concrete sculptures of biblical and political figures – he even built his own mausoleum where his nearly century-old corpse is still on display.

 Admire works by self-taught creators at the Grassroots Arts Center, also in Lucas.

 Hike Little Jerusalem Badlands State Park, opened only in 2019, where otherworldly limestone columns rise like grand temples from the flat plains.

 Visit tiny Nicodemus, founded by formerly enslaved people in 1877 as the first Black town west of the Mississippi. It's still a living community, and the National Park Service has restored and reopened the town hall and church.

Opposite: The wide prairies of Kansas have a slow-burning beauty. **Above, left:** Bowl Plaza in Lucas is an flashy public restroom; **right**: hiking the trails of Little Jerusalem Badlands

181

Opposite: The palatial interior of Union Station in Kansas City

Kansas City Missouri

**SPORTS, CULTURE, ART AND HISTORY:
THE HEART OF AMERICA IS BEATING LOUDER THAN EVER**

easy to slip into local life even on a short visit. And no, those aren't tourists you see wearing the ubiquitous KC-in-a-heart tees – those are proud Kansas Citians.

Kansas City's artsy attitude and growing indie scene of hip local shops, resurrected distilleries and craft beer culture occasionally lean toward Portland, and the live music scene – jazz in particular – puts it on stage with Nashville, though those cities are more commonly included on US travelers' itineraries. In-the-know sports fanatics and unabashed barbecue gluttons aren't the only ones who can find the soul of Kansas City.

GO IF YOU LIKE…
- 🤍 *Nashville*
- 🤍 *Portland*
- 🤍 *sports*
- 🤍 *museums and galleries*
- 🤍 *live music*
- 🤍 *barbecue*

H iding in plain sight in the middle of the US, Kansas City has been underappreciated for years. Ignore any naysayers who dismiss it as the unofficial capital of 'flyover country' – Kansas City is tentatively tiptoeing toward the spotlight and should not be missed.

Perhaps constrained by a classically humble Midwest mindset, KC has tons to brag about but would rather let travelers discover for themselves what makes the Heart of America tick. Its laid-back vibe means that it's

Why go to Kansas City?

With nearly as many fountains as Rome and more barbecue joints than you can shake a spit at, Kansas City hits the sweet spot: enough to explore over a weekend and attractions that are rarely packed. Sports remain a big draw, and not just the obvious ones. The world's first stadium purpose-built for a women's sports team is opening for the Kansas City Current soccer club in 2024, and KC was selected to host some of the 2026 World Cup matches.

In addition to country-leading museums and art galleries, KC is tackling new projects to revitalize forgotten parts of town. Walt Disney took drawing classes at the Kansas City Art Institute and founded his first business here, Laugh-O-Gram Studio, which a local group has received $2 million to renovate. An abandoned railway bridge 40 feet over the Kansas River is being transformed into an entertainment district slated to open in 2024.

GETTING THERE

Kansas City opened a new state-of-the-art airport terminal in 2023, decked out in city-centric commissioned art, local restaurants – yes, you can finally get barbecue while waiting for your flight – and all the tech trimmings, including USB-C sockets and all-gender bathrooms with lights indicating which stalls are free. Amtrak trains still pull into the grand Union Station, opened in 1914, from St Louis, Chicago and Los Angeles.

WHEN TO GO

Apr – Jun, Sep & Oct

The Midwest sees extreme temperatures on both sides of the scale, so visit in spring or fall to enjoy the city to the fullest. Spring can bring tornadoes and severe thunderstorms.

AMAZING CROWD-FREE EXPERIENCES

 Admire the globe-trotting collection of the Nelson-Atkins Museum of Art – which wouldn't be out of place in a city much larger than KC – for free.

 **Understand the significance of the Great War** at the National World War I Museum, which Congress designated as the country's official WWI museum and memorial.

 Explore Kansas City's hub of Black culture at 18th and Vine, a historic district noted as a birthplace of jazz that's home to the Negro Leagues Baseball Museum and Missouri's first Black-owned brewery.

 Sample the spirits of Kansas City at J Rieger, the first distillery to open since Prohibition.

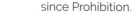 **Appreciate the elegant architecture of Union Station,** a Beaux-Arts beauty with huge chandeliers and ornate ceilings. The station also houses a science museum, theater, planetarium and temporary exhibitions.

  Get sauced at Joe's Kansas City Bar-B-Que, a barbecue spot inside a working gas station that's served presidents and celebrities.

FIRST-TIME TIPS

<u>*Know whether you're in Kansas or Missouri*</u>*. Kansas City spans both states, and neither likes being called the other. Don't make the same mistake that many musicians and former presidents have by boldly announcing which state you're in and getting it wrong.*

Look at the menu of barbecue restaurants online <u>before you go</u>. Some places, such as Gates, yell for your order as soon as you walk in the door.

Kansas City's public transportation network isn't extensive, but it is <u>free to ride</u>. The 2-mile-long streetcar line that runs through downtown is best for visitors.

Top: Sports history at the Negro Leagues Baseball Museum; **bottom**: slow-smoked barbecue with all the trimmings

Shawnee National Forest Illinois

UNDEREXPLORED FORESTS, CANYONS AND THE GREAT SNAKE MIGRATION

WISCONSIN

IOWA

ILLINOIS

MISSOURI

Shawnee National Forest

At the southern tip of Illinois, nestled between the Ohio River and the mighty Mississippi, lies the 280,000-acre Shawnee National Forest, a unique ecological crossroads. Nowhere else in the United States can hikers trek through six different ecosystems in one day, including lush oak-hickory forests, flourishing wetlands, wide-open prairie, windswept bluffs and deep canyons.

More than 320 million years ago, the wind and rain began chiseling away at the large sedimentary rock deposits here, creating the massive sandstone formations of the forest's Garden of the Gods, which was recently featured as part of the US Mint's America the Beautiful quarter series.

The first wine trail in Illinois wends through the forest, too. Eleven wineries, each one with its own style and winemaking technique, dot the 40-mile route and are part of a popular scenic drive. Wildlife enthusiasts should keep an eye out for armadillos, bald eagles, bobcats, red-tailed hawks, red foxes and over 250 bird species. And some say that the legendary Bigfoot wanders the forest as well…

GO IF YOU LIKE…
- 💜 *wine*
- 🩶 *hiking*
- 🩶 *rock climbing*
- 💜 *Native American history*

187

Why go to Shawnee National Forest?

With over four hundred miles of trails, there's a hike for every type of outdoor enthusiast at Shawnee National Forest. One of the biggest draws is the moderately challenging River to River Trail. Leading from the Ohio River to the Mississippi, this 160-mile trail traverses wetlands, upland forests, grasslands and bluffs. The Little Grand Canyon Trail winds for 3 miles past waterfalls and incredible rock formations to the base of a canyon smaller in scale than Arizona's Big Ditch, but no less awe-inspiring.

For outdoor enthusiasts who want to pair fine wines with a scenic hike, the Southern Illinois Wine Trail loops through the rolling hills of Illinois's first designated grape-growing region, inviting hikers to sip and savor nature. The region's high elevation and location between two major rivers creates an ideal weather-resistant climate that produces some of the highest-quality grapes in the United States.

GETTING THERE

Shawnee National Forest spans the southernmost part of Illinois and is about 150 miles southeast of St Louis, Missouri. The closest major airport, Lambert International Airport (St Louis), is connected to the region via I-64 and I-57. Amtrak rail service runs from St Louis to Carbondale, Illinois, the largest town adjacent to the park and home of Southern Illinois University.

WHEN TO GO

Sep & Oct

Thanks to its fairly mild weather, Shawnee National Forest can be enjoyed almost any time of the year. Fall is the highlight, though, when the air is crisp and the trees are a riot of color.

FIRST-TIME TIPS

Cell reception is nonexistent in many parts of Shawnee National Forest, so bring a map, compass or GPS device, or download an off-line app like AllTrails or CalTopo to your phone.

Heavy rainfall may cause rivers and streams to rise quickly and stay elevated for days afterward, causing certain roads and trails to become impassable. Be aware of weather conditions before setting off into the forest.

Watch where you step. Over 20 types of snake live in the Shawnee National Forest, including three venomous species: the copperhead, cottonmouth (water moccasin) and timber rattlesnake.

AMAZING CROWD-FREE EXPERIENCES

 Explore Cave in Rock, the late 18th-century hideout of many outlaws and river pirates.

 Witness the biannual snake migration along the 2.7-mile Snake Road. In spring, thousands of snakes and amphibians slither out of the forest's limestone bluffs and into LaRue Swamp. In the fall, they head in the opposite direction, as they hibernate each winter at the base of the dry limestone cliffs.

 Hike the easy trail to Camel Rock (.5 mile), located in the Garden of the Gods wilderness area.

 Climb inside the Iron Furnace. From 1837 through 1967, this massive stone furnace produced nine tons of iron a day.

 Visit the Native American village site situated atop Millstone Bluff. A .75-mile trail leads to the archeological site, which dates to between 600 to 900 CE.

 Look for deer, beavers, muskrats and bobcats along the 3.1-mile Panther Den Wilderness Area loop trail.

Opposite, left: Timber rattlesnakes are one of Shawnee's more than 20 snake species; **right**: walking trails wind through the Garden of the Gods. **Below**: Illinois' only remaining iron furnace structure

Columbus Indiana

UNEXPECTED LIVING MUSEUM OF MODERNIST ARCHITECTURE AMID FIELDS OF CORN

ILLINOIS

INDIANA

OHIO

Columbus

KENTUCKY

If you're not an architect – or at least a fervent architecture enthusiast – you probably haven't heard of Columbus, Indiana. Or maybe you hadn't until you saw the 2017 independent film, *Columbus*, starring Haley Lu Richardson. After all, there are people from Indiana who don't know a thing about it. Located 46 miles south of Indianapolis, Columbus is flanked by typical Midwestern surrounds (cornfields, red barns and basketball hoops in every driveway) but this small Hoosier town is anything but ordinary. Spearheaded in the 1940s by American industrial visionary J Erwin Miller, Columbus and its leading corporation, the Miller-led Fortune 500 engineering firm Cummins, commissioned some of the world's most revered 20th-century masters to design many of its public and private buildings. More than 70 notable buildings and public art installations dot the city like interactive exhibits in an outdoor design museum. World-class architects, including Eliel Saarinen, Eero Saarinen, Kevin Roche, IM Pei, Harry Weese and Deborah Berke, have turned a John Mellencamp small town into an internationally renowned architectural hotbed.

GO IF YOU LIKE...
- *mid-century modern architecture*
- *small-town America*
- *historic homes*
- *public art*
- *National Historic Landmarks*

Why go to Columbus?

As you roll into Indiana's 20th-largest city, nothing immediately seems amiss. Small Midwestern towns tend toward a certain aesthetic, and at first glance Columbus appears to aspire to similar ambitions. And then, from out of nowhere, Columbus unexpectedly reveals itself as a living museum of mid-century modern architecture. Simple civic buildings that normally wouldn't deserve a fleeting glance (the post office, fire stations, banks) stop you in your tracks. The First Christian Church, designed by Eliel Saarinen, was one of the first modernist religious buildings in the country. The Cleo Rogers Memorial Library is an assortment of clean-lined perfection by IM Pei. Nearly every building in town is Instagrammable (no filter required). There are few cities like it, if any, in the United States or beyond. Frank Lloyd Wright's unrealized Broadacre City might have looked something like this, but we'll never know.

FIRST-TIME TIPS

Resist the vacation rentals and typical chain hotels. Instead, stay at the historic Inn at Irwin Gardens (irwingardens.com), a Victorian mansion with Edwardian furnishings and Italianate gardens.

Columbus's compact downtown is home to 15 of the town's 70 architectural gems, but don't miss eye-catching constructions further afield, including Robert Venturi's Fire Station No 4 and Eero Saarinen's North Christian Church.

There is free parking at Mill Race Park, a half-mile walk to the Columbus Visitors Center and other downtown attractions.

Book ahead for a meal and exquisite cocktails at New American standout Henry Social Club.

GETTING THERE

Indianapolis International Airport is located 55 miles northwest of Columbus. The easiest way to reach the city is by car, but Barons Bus (ride.baronsbus.com) departs daily at 4:20pm from Greyhound's Indianapolis Bus Station for the one-hour ride to Columbus.

WHEN TO GO

Apr, May, Sep, Oct

Avoid the muggy Midwestern summer by visiting Columbus in the spring or fall, when temps are cool but pleasant.

Opposite: The Cleo Rogers Memorial Library is a brick and limestone sanctuary. **Left:** Bold Columbus signs set the scene for this design-obsessed city

AMAZING CROWD-FREE EXPERIENCES

 Explore downtown's architectural standouts on a self-guided tour. Pick up a guide for $3 at the Columbus Visitors Center.

 Take a tour of the Miller House and Garden. J Erwin Miller's private home is one of the most important mid-century modern residences in the US.

 Treat yourself to a hand-dipped sundae at Zaharakos Ice Cream. This old-fashioned ice cream parlor has been churning out sweet treats since 1900.

 Climb the observation tower at Mill Race Park. The 84-foot-high structure has a panoramic view over downtown and the city's Flatrock and Driftwood Rivers.

 Reconnoiter the best photo angle inside Cleo Rogers Memorial Library. IM Pei's stunning public library reveals an endless arsenal of clean-lined photo-ops.

 Indulge in Hazy IPAs and Fruited Berliners at 450 North Brewing Co. Leave downtown behind for craft beers on a local family farm.

Isle Royale National Park Michigan

A PRISTINE WILDERNESS FOR HIKING, KAYAKING AND MARVELING AT MOOSE

day – which means the unspoiled forest is all yours. There are no roads, just 165 miles of hiking trails, 36 rustic campgrounds, two no-frills cabins and one lodge. It's certainly the place to go for peace and quiet. And moose and wolves. The island's isolation has led to a unique ecosystem for the two animals, which is now the subject of the longest-running predator-prey study in the world. At last count around one thousand moose and 30 wolves prowled the park. Sightings, especially of the big brown skinny-legged twig eaters, are practically guaranteed.

GO IF YOU LIKE...
- *solitude*
- *moose sightings*
- *hiking*
- *wilderness adventures*
- *canoeing or kayaking*
- *Acadia National Park*

Morning fog wisps over the lake. You hear sloshing on the shore and see a moose plop in for a drink. A loon calls – or is that the howl of a wolf? Either is probable on Isle Royale, one of the least-visited national parks in the United States.

The 45-mile-long island floats on its lonesome in Lake Superior, between Michigan and Minnesota. Only 25,000 visitors per year make the journey – fewer than Acadia National Park gets on a single summer

Why go to Isle Royale National Park?

There are so few places in North America that aren't Instagrammed to death. Isle Royale is one of them, not only because it requires serious work to get there (by wave-tossed ferry or windblown seaplane), but also because there is neither cell phone service nor wi-fi on the island. You're forced to unplug and be present in the moment as you hike trails lined with wild thimbleberries, camp under the star-spangled sky and listen for foxes and beavers tramping through the woods.

The park is working to restore the island's 19th-century lighthouses, historic copper mining sites and abandoned fishing villages, so these will add to the scene in coming years. For now, it's all about strapping on a backpack, setting out on foot or by canoe or kayak, and immersing yourself in a pristine patch of wilderness where the moose outnumber humans. It's about as untouched as you'll get.

GETTING THERE

Ferries to Isle Royale depart from Houghton, Michigan (six hours); Copper Harbor, Michigan (3½ hours); and Grand Portage, Minnesota (90 minutes). Seaplanes are faster but more expensive, departing from Houghton (35 minutes) and Grand Marais, Minnesota (45 minutes). The closest main airports are Chicago O'Hare (with connections to Houghton) and Duluth International (a 150-mile drive from Grand Portage).

WHEN TO GO

mid-Apr – Oct

The park is busiest from mid-June through early September. This is also when insects can be a bother. Mid-September through October is good for fall colors, though the weather can be unpredictable. The park closes November through mid-April due to extreme conditions.

© F. SETIAWAN / SHUTTERSTOCK, © STEVE LAGRECA / SHUTTERSTOCK, © MATT CHAMPLIN / GETTY IMAGES

FIRST-TIME TIPS

Make ferry bookings and lodge reservations as soon as possible. While Isle Royale gets few visitors, slots are still limited.

Anyone not staying at the lodge needs to bring their own tent, camping stove, sleeping bag, food and water filter. You can't buy supplies on the island.

Campsites are first come, first served for parties of six or fewer. Camping fees are included in the $7 daily entrance fee.

Fog, storms, wind and other wild weather mean ferry and seaplane cancellations are common. Be sure to bring extra supplies, just in case.

AMAZING CROWD-FREE EXPERIENCES

 Backpack the 42-mile Greenstone Ridge Trail, an epic trek that spans the island and pays off big with forest solitude and fab lookouts over the wave-based coast.

 Mingle with moose. It's common to see them feeding at Washington Creek in Windigo, Hidden Lake near Rock Harbor and other inland watering holes.

 Gaze into the incredibly dark sky. There's no light pollution, and you might even glimpse the northern lights.

 Hike the Stoll Trail, a short loop that begins at Rock Harbor Lodge and meanders through old-growth forest and along dramatic shoreline bluffs.

 Canoe or kayak the inland lakes. Start at Belle Isle and glide through protected bays en route to Rock Harbor.

 Dive the icy waters to explore the wrecks of 10 ships that sank during the copper and silver booms of the late 1800s.

Clockwise from top: A seaplane arriving at Isle Royale; red foxes are common on walking trails; the 1855 Rock Harbor Lighthouse is a popular stop

Opposite: Graphic
lettering by Doris Shlayn
at the Columbus College
of Art and Design

Columbus Ohio

A MIDWESTERN CULTURE HUB WITH AN INTERNATIONAL FEEL

MICHIGAN

PENNSYLVANIA

Columbus

INDIANA

OHIO

KENTUCKY

L et's face it. With the exception of Chicago, the Midwest is often overlooked when it comes to travel plans. But those who skip over this broad swathe of country are missing out on a fascinating city full of surprises: Columbus, Ohio.

While Columbus frequently plays host to sports fans thanks to the massive Ohio State University, it also functions as Ohio's art hub, attracting all manner of creatives – the city is home to the third-highest

concentration of fashion designers in the country, trailing only New York City and Los Angeles. Workshops, studios and galleries pepper the city, and top-tier cultural centers like the Wexner Center for the Arts, the Columbus College of Art and Design and the Columbus Museum of Art showcase visual art, performance art, film and more.

Columbus has a large immigrant community, giving the Arch City a distinctly international feel, and it's also home to a very visible LGBTIQ+ community, with pride flags prominently waving throughout the city year-round.

GO IF YOU LIKE...
- 🤍 *foodie experiences*
- 🤍 *historical architecture*
- 🤍 *art and fashion*
- 🤍 *LGBTIQ+ community*
- 🤍 *international eats*
- 🤍 *shopping*

199

Why go to Columbus?

Creativity is the name of the game in Columbus, and this ethos manifests in every part of the city. In Short North, discover shops selling everything from custom stationary to sequined jackets to imported treasures from around the world, and then pop into the Ginger Rabbit lounge for cocktails and jazz. In German Village, explore the labyrinthine Book Loft (32 rooms worth of books) and snag an immaculate pastry from Fox in the Snow Cafe.

Fashion shows and art exhibitions are commonplace – visit designers in their studios as part of Fashion Night Out and discover emerging talent at Columbus Fashion Week. And don't miss the High Ball in October, an extravagant runway event focused on costume couture.

Foodies will also be overwhelmed with top-tier options throughout the city. Sample masterpieces of texture and design at Veritas, dive into plates of colorful Filipino dishes at Bonifacio or relish in thoughtful dishes at award-winning Chapmans Eat Market.

FIRST-TIME TIPS

Columbus is home to _Ohio State University_, a huge institution with over 60,000 students – check the calendar for big university events before booking.

Many of Columbus' neighborhoods are walkable (particularly Short North and German Village), but _you'll need a car_ to travel between them.

Columbus is relatively flat, which makes it bikeable! Bring your own or use the city's _bikeshare system CoGo_ – a single trip is $2.25.

AMAZING CROWD-FREE EXPERIENCES

 Wander the brick sidewalks of German Village and snag a sausage from Schmidt's before perusing the labyrinthine Book Loft, a bookstore with 32 rooms.

 Hop into a kayak and paddle the Scioto River, accessible from several put-ins near downtown.

 For international eats, dig into a heaping plate of kebabs and saffron rice at Charmy's Persian Taste or wander the many options at North Market – Indian, Polish, Nepalese and Somali cuisine are all on offer.

 Catch a show at one of Columbus' many drag bars – District West and Boscoe's are good bets. Be sure to bring those dollars to tip the queens (and kings)!

 Stay in Columbus' Art Deco gem, Hotel LeVeque, which at the time of completion in 1927 was the highest building between Chicago and New York City.

 Dig into vegan masterpieces like BBQ pulled-mushroom sandwiches and breakfast burritos with coconut bacon – then shop for indie books at Two Dollar Radio Headquarters.

Right: Sunset adds shimmer to downtown Columbus; **below:** German comfort food at Schmidt's Sausage Haus

GETTING THERE

Columbus' airport has a large number of domestic connections, so most folks will be able to fly right into the city without having to worry about an additional transfer; international travelers will need to fly into a larger city like NYC or Atlanta first. Columbus is well served by highways, with the other closest hubs being Dayton and Cincinnati.

WHEN TO GO

Mar – Nov

Spring, summer and fall are all great times to visit thanks to mild weather, but winters are often cold and snowy.

Hocking Hills Ohio

SCENERY AND SERENITY IN OHIO'S HIDDEN HILLS

MICHIGAN

PENNSYLVANIA

OHIO

INDIANA

Hocking Hills State Park

KENTUCKY

country. Hiking is plentiful and trails reveal a network of clear-blue waterfalls, old-growth forests and sandstone arches and outcroppings. Above, the skies are dark, giving stargazers front-row seats to the cosmos.

But as beautiful as Hocking Hills is, it's more than an outdoor destination. Creatives have made their way here, painting, glassblowing, blacksmithing and sculpting in the quiet hollows. This cultural richness has also spilled over into the hospitality sector, with unique accommodations hosting weekend getaways and longer retreats alike.

GO IF YOU LIKE...
- *unique rock formations*
- *cozy accommodations*
- *Appalachia*
- *local art*
- *dark skies*
- *weekend getaways*

The majority of Ohio was scraped clean by a massive glacier millions of years ago, but the giant mass eventually stopped its onward slog, leaving today's Hocking Hills, an undulating region of southeastern Ohio that looks more akin to its mountainous neighbors than the rest of the state.

Here, time and erosion have created wave-like cliffs, giant boulder fields and some of the deepest recess caves in the eastern part of the

Why go to Hocking Hills?

The pace is slow in Hocking Hills, and it's perfect for visitors who want to take it easy. Activity-wise, outdoor adventure experiences are numerous and accessible – marvel at the stunning Old Man's Cave and Rock House, or take a relaxing float on Logan Lake. Looking for culture? Jack Pine Studio hosts a Glass Garden Festival in the spring and a Glass Pumpkin Festival in the fall, taking its blown-glass creations outdoors. Maker and artisan classes also abound.

But perhaps the most intriguing aspect of Hocking Hills is the assortment of interesting places to stay. Get the best sleep of your life in an underground hobbit house – complete with firewood-warmed hot tubs – at Magical Earth Retreat, or stay in a luxurious house built into a recess cave at Dunlap Hollow. The Inn and Spa at Cedar Falls offers the chance to sleep in a geodesic dome or a traditional cabin, too.

GETTING THERE

Hocking Hills is only accessible by car, though the journey is a picturesque one once you start getting close to your destination – it's a one-hour drive from Columbus and a two-hour drive from Cincinnati.

WHEN TO GO

Year-round

Spring, summer and fall are prime for hikers and adventurers, while winter is an amazing time to cozy up in one of the region's comfy inns and admire the snowy landscape beside a fire.

FIRST-TIME TIPS

While Hocking Hills is off the beaten path for many, it can still get busy with locals on summer weekends. Book ahead or opt for a visit during the week.

Cell service is unreliable throughout Hocking Hills, so download all directions beforehand. If hiking, download an app like AllTrails or CalTopo.

The region's roads are narrow and curvy, and some turns aren't well marked. Drive slowly.

Hiking paths can be hilly and rocky, so wear appropriate footwear.

AMAZING CROWD-FREE EXPERIENCES

 Watch glass being blown into unique organic shapes at the enchanting Jack Pine Studio. Book a class or peruse the impressive collection of pieces for sale.

 Go rappelling or rock climbing amid Hocking Hills' unique geological formations with High Rock Adventures.

 Drink award-winning beer at Little Fish Brewery. It's brewed with Ohio-grown ingredients at the sustainability-focused facility powered by solar and wind technology.

 Attend a star-gazing event at the John Glenn Astronomy Park and learn all about the cosmos. Bring a camera and tripod to snap some excellent extraterrestrial shots.

 Sample dozens of apple varieties at Laurelville Fruit Farm and quench your thirst with a refreshing apple cider slushie.

 Book a spa day at one of the several wellness centers across Hocking Hills. You can even spend an afternoon in a salt cave to absorb the benefits of Himalayan salt.

Above: The Milky Way glittering above Lake Logan. **Below:** Rocks framing snow-covered trees in Hocking Hills

This spread:
Everglades National Park, Florida

Southeast
USA

Opposite: Crawfish boils are one of Lafayette's irresistible food experiences

Lafayette Louisiana

CAJUN AND CREOLE CULTURE IN THE HEART OF LOUISIANA

ARKANSAS

MISSISSIPPI

LOUISIANA

TEXAS

Lafayette

flamboyant chicken chases during Mardi Gras – just one event on a full calendar.

If you love to eat, hop from one delicious Lafayette restaurant to the next for some of the best gumbo, po' boys and boudin anywhere outside a *maw maw*'s kitchen. And a new crop of restaurants preaching the gospel of local foodways is mixing up the pot in clever, tasty ways.

Lafayette calls itself the happiest city in America, and while we can't verify that, it's awfully hard to visit without a smile on your face.

GO IF YOU LIKE...
- *New Orleans*
- *history*
- *French and Creole*
- *music and dancing*
- *spiced food*
- *drive-through daiquiris*

N ew Orleans gets plenty of visitors, but a trip into central Louisiana provides the chance to experience one of the most culturally rich small towns in the US. In the heart of Acadiana, aka Cajun Country, Lafayette celebrates the Cajuns and Creoles who resiliently adapted to life in the swamp. Boogie to Cajun and zydeco music in a lively dance hall or at the Festival Acadiens et Créoles, a music festival that recently celebrated its 50th year. And speaking of dancing, Lafayette hosts

Why go to Lafayette?

Lafayette is undergoing a cultural renaissance as well as an urban one, with a reinvigorated, walkable downtown core. A government proposal may also make it more bikeable, with plans to develop nearly 50 miles of bike lanes and trails that would connect 16 surrounding communities.

The Cajuns have traditionally received more attention than the Creoles, but that's starting to change with the new Creole-centric Maison Freetown cultural center and museum. And everyone's welcome to join Black cowboys at a Creole trail ride in surrounding towns.

Everywhere you turn there seems to be a new restaurant in Lafayette. Try Five Mile Eatery for farm-to-table comfort food and Parc de Oaks Food Truck Park for a buffet of spicy soul food. For something in rather than out of the pot, have a coffee while learning how to take care of your home foliage at Coffeeweed Cottage's plant bar.

GETTING THERE

Lafayette has a regional airport, but it's a fun and scenic road trip along the I-10 from New Orleans (135 miles away) or Houston (217 miles). Hwy 90 is a great option if you have more time as it skips through small towns along the Atchafalaya River. Alternatively, there are bus and Amtrak train connections to both major cities.

WHEN TO GO

Mar – May

Springtime is festival season in Lafayette and also when the weather is most pleasant, with average temps in the 70s. Summertime is the rainy season and temperatures can be scorching hot.

AMAZING CROWD-FREE EXPERIENCES

 Watch locals chase live chickens while dressed in flamboyant fringed costumes at Lafayette's unique Mardi Gras, a tradition that hails from Europe.

 Peruse the latest English- and French-language titles at Beausoleil Books, and stay from 6pm to late at the Whisper Room to shop with booze in hand.

 Kayak around cypress trees on the lookout for alligators in Lake Martin swamp.

 Catch crawfish the old-fashioned way using a hand net, then boil them yourself at Crawfish Haven, which is also a B&B.

 Bounce in a wagon to zydeco and hip-hop music with Black cowboys on horseback at a Creole trail ride every weekend in towns around Lafayette.

 Attend a secret supper show in the garden at Maison Madeleine B&B featuring Grammy award–winning musicians and James Beard–nominated chefs from the South.

Clockwise from top: Settler life at the Acadian Village; cypress trees rising from marshland; alligators lurk in Lafayette's swamps.

Opposite: Wooden cabin on the outskirts of Clarksdale

Clarksdale Mississippi

THE BIRTHPLACE OF THE BLUES MEETS SOME OF THE SOUTH'S BEST SOUL FOOD

TENNESSEE

ARKANSAS

Clarksdale

ALABAMA

MISSISSIPPI

LOUISIANA

We challenge you to name a small town that has made a larger contribution to American music than Clarksdale, Mississippi. This dusty Delta crossroads on the banks of the Sunflower River is the birthplace of blues – a genre inspired by African rhythms, plantation songs and church hymns. Blues fused with country and jazz to form rock 'n' roll, whose first song, 'Rocket 88,' was written and rehearsed by Ike Turner and Jackie Brenston in the basement of Clarksdale's (now closed) Riverside Hotel. Clarksdale is where Sam Cooke, the masterful voice behind Civil Rights anthem 'A Change Is Gonna Come' 'was born by the river.' It's also where Muddy Waters first recorded and Robert Johnson sold his soul to the devil in exchange for his guitar prowess – or so the story goes.

Yet Clarksdale is often skipped in lieu of other cities like Memphis, Nashville, New Orleans and Chicago – and that's a shame, because it doesn't get more authentic than Clarksdale. Fortunately, a passionate group of locals and immigrants are making sure it stays that way.

GO IF YOU LIKE...
- ♥ *Memphis and Nashville*
- ♥ *soul music*
- ♥ *soul food*
- ♥ *culture and history*
- ♥ *road trips*
- ♥ *authenticity*

213

Why go to Clarksdale?

For decades, Clarksdale was left to decay – racial violence and new economic opportunities spurred the decades-long Great Migration north. But in recent years, Clarksdale's downtown strip has been given a shot of life-saving medicine. You can now see live music seven days a week at mythological venues and juke joints like Red's Lounge, Bluesberry Cafe and Ground Zero Blues Club, co-owned by actor Morgan Freeman. There are more than a dozen annual music festivals, including April's Juke Joint Festival, May's Women in Blues Festival and August's Sunflower River Blues and Gospel Festival, which has been going strong for more than 30 years. Clarksdale has new hotels in restored buildings like the Travelers Hotel, which was started by a local nonprofit cooperative, and its first dorms at Auberge Clarksdale Hostel. New isn't always better, of course: Clarksdale still has some of the finest soul food in the South.

GETTING THERE

Clarksdale is best visited on a music pilgrimage from New Orleans to Memphis, passing through the Mississippi Delta. Along the way, you'll get to cruise the winding Natchez Trace Parkway and can hop around to signposted sites on the Mississippi Blues and Civil Rights trails. It's easily reached from I-55.

WHEN TO GO

Apr – May

Go in the spring to see the Juke Joint and Women in Blues festivals before the summer heat and hurricane season hit.

Above, left: Cotton fields in bloom; **right**: live music at Red's Blues Club. **Opposite:** The Crossroads between Highways 61 and 49 is legendary in blues lore

FIRST-TIME TIPS

Visit the recently updated <u>Delta Blues Museum</u> in a 1918 railroad depot for the run-down on Mississippi's treasured music history.

Brush up on music by <u>local legends</u> Sam Cooke, Muddy Waters, Ike Turner and Robert Johnson, and hip-hop icons Rick Ross and Nate Dogg.

Shop for local books, T-shirts, artwork, vinyl and CDs at <u>Cat Head</u> and chat with passionate Ohio-born owner Roger Stolle.

Consult the Cat Head's website (cathead.biz) for a detailed list of <u>weekly concerts</u> and annual festivals – it's updated monthly.

Visit <u>Robert Johnson's crossroads</u> at Desoto Ave and N State St.

AMAZING CROWD-FREE EXPERIENCES

 Feel your face melt in front of an electric guitar at an intimate juke joint or restaurant.

 Order dripping tamales and wing tips from the drive-through at Hick's BBQ and eat fried catfish at Lebanese-owned Rest Haven, both of which have been open for over 50 years.

 Dance with other passionate music lovers at a festival like the nearby Bentonia Blues Festival, which has been running for more than half a century.

 Shop for local tchotchkes and plants at one of Clarksdale's coolest new shops, Collective Seed & Supply Co, launched by the same nonprofit as Travelers Hotel.

 Canoe the Mississippi River on an expedition with local tour operator Quapaw Canoe Company, which also runs apprenticeships for Clarksdale youth.

 Road trip to the abandoned juke joint Po' Monkey and still-active Blue Front Cafe and imagine how fun they must've been in their heyday.

Lexington Kentucky

A QUINTESSENTIALLY KENTUCKY CITY WITH AN ARTSY EDGE

When it comes to tourism, Kentucky is best known for two things: bourbon and the Kentucky Derby, both headquartered in the bustling river city of Louisville. While Derby City is worth a visit, Louisville's sister city Lexington sits just an hour and a half east and is largely overlooked. A pity, because this cozy town harbors a robust creative spirit. If you want a destination that feels both forward-thinking and essentially Kentucky, this is your stop.

Situated smack-dab in the heart of horse country, Lexington is objectively gorgeous – rolling green hills encircle two universities and a historic downtown that buzzes with restaurants, galleries and bars. Sounds like any mid-sized city, right?

But let's add a dash of spice: top-tier bourbon bars, edgy large-scale murals (like, *really* big), abandoned distilleries that have been revamped into thriving entertainment districts, a historic art-house movie theater and excellent hiking through one of the country's oldest gorges just a short drive away.

GO IF YOU LIKE...

- 🩶 *Louisville*
- 🩶 *bourbon*
- 🩶 *horses*
- 🩶 *street art*
- 🩶 *down-home food*
- 🩶 *picturesque countryside*

Why go to Lexington?

Lexington has accomplished something that not many other cities have been able to do: it has evolved with the times without losing its soul. Each neighborhood has its own distinct feel – snag local eats and suds in refurbished historic buildings along Jefferson St; catch an indie musician or a burlesque show at North Limestone's longtime quirky dive Al's Bar; or sip cider on Manchester St while overlooking Town Branch, a waterway essential to Lexington's founding.

But Lexington isn't stuck in its small-town ways. It also has an inclusive atmosphere and diverse social experiences. It has a very active LGBTIQ+ community – June hums with Pride events and local organizations lead queer history tours through the city. At the Festival Latino de Lexington in September, downtown comes alive with music, food and cultural activities, and the organization Black Soil Kentucky hosts farm-to-table dinners and farm tours that highlight Black-owned businesses.

GETTING THERE

Lexington has a small airport that has flights to and from several cities in the Midwest and East. The main driving thoroughfares to Lexington are I-75, I-64, and the Bluegrass Parkway. It's a 1½-hour drive to both Louisville and Cincinnati.

WHEN TO GO

Mar – Nov

The Horse Capital of the World is a year-round destination, but the city comes alive with events – and excellent weather – in the spring and fall. Summer is warm but not unbearable and winters are generally mild.

AMAZING CROWD-FREE EXPERIENCES

 Spend an afternoon driving through the horse farms on the city's outskirts, or book a tour at local farms and equine care centers.

 Book a tour to some of the 15 distilleries that lie within 45 miles of Lexington; many businesses provide transportation between distilleries.

 Explore the Distillery District on Manchester Street, home to restaurants, cocktail bars, a brewery, a cidery, music venues and more.

 Sip German beer from Blue Stallion and sample locally grown vegan eats at Kentucky Native Cafe, a historic greenhouse turned epic outdoor eatery.

 Catch the Woodland Art Fair in August, an artistic extravaganza highlighting Kentucky makers and artisans.

 Learn about Kentucky's equine history at the Kentucky Horse Park. Watch a horse show, tour barns and meet horses of all breeds, while taking in the scenery.

Clockwise from below left: Distilleries serve a vast bourbon selection; the Kentucky Derby is the state's best-known event; Louis Armstrong beaming from a mural

Chattanooga Tennessee

THE SOUTHEAST'S BEST UNDER-THE-RADAR CITY

W hen it comes to outdoorsy cities in the United States, places like Denver, Asheville and Portland often come to mind. But you're missing out on Chattanooga, the little Tennessee town that became part of the American lexicon thanks to its signature choo choo and some of the most recognizable kitsch attractions in the country (Rock City, anyone?). While it may have gotten onto the tourism map with its arguably niche attractions, this city-that-could has blossomed into a verifiable outdoor haven with a sustainable mindset.

Chattanooga sits within the Appalachian foothills and is home to some of the best rock climbing in the country. Visitors will also find themselves conveniently situated close to other outdoor pursuits, like water sports and hiking. Chattanooga has also put substantial effort into developing its food and art scenes, so you'll be eating well and enjoying plenty of culture to boot.

GO IF YOU LIKE...
- 🖤 *Asheville*
- 🖤 *American kitsch*
- 🖤 *water sports*
- 🖤 *rock climbing*
- 🖤 *farm-to-table food*
- 🖤 *music*

Why go to Chattanooga?

Chattanooga offers all the hallmarks of a great adventure getaway – close proximity to outdoor attractions, excellent food and drink, plenty of family activities – all without feeling overrun or inauthentic.

Take a paddleboarding trip down the Tennessee River, which loops lazily through the city, or head just out of city limits to the more energetic Ocoee River. The Tennessee Wall is the city's big rock-climbing highlight, but there are several other world-class spots here. And while it's technically indoors, Chattanooga is home to one of the best aquariums in this part of the country.

Environmental and social responsibility is clearly on display here, too. Restaurants like the Flying Squirrel run resource-aware food programs, while organizations like TrailblazUS focus on creating an inclusive outdoor community. The Hunter Museum of American Art stages exhibits with important historical and social context, and local organic farms offer tours to educate folks on the importance of Slow Food.

Below: Friends enjoy Champy's famous fried chicken
Opposite: Rock climbing the Tennessee Wall

FIRST-TIME TIPS

Parking in downtown Chattanooga is limited and expensive. If you're coming from outside of downtown, opt for a rideshare. Within downtown, make use of the free electric shuttle.

....

Chattanooga is a convenient hub for exploring north Georgia. Hop over the border for more great outdoor attractions like Cloudland Canyon, as well as Civil War historical sites including the Chickamauga Battlefield.

....

Check out Visit Chattanooga (visitchattanooga.com) for deals and coupons to the city's attractions and restaurants.

....

If visiting Chattanooga's most touristy attractions – Ruby Falls, Rock City, or the aquarium – try to go during off-peak hours during the week.

GETTING THERE

Chattanooga is located in south-central Tennessee and has a small airport that connects to major domestic hubs, the closest of which is Atlanta. Otherwise, Chattanooga is easily accessible from two of the region's major highways – I-24 and 1-75. Atlanta is a two-hour drive; Nashville is three.

WHEN TO GO

Year-round

Spring and summer are the best times to visit if you plan on participating in watersports, but fall and winter give visitors a break from the heat and offer excellent hiking weather.

AMAZING CROWD-FREE EXPERIENCES

 Learn about Chattanooga's lengthy and influential Black history at the Bessie Smith Cultural Center and Chattanooga African American Museum.

 Visit the museum at the Songbirds Foundation to explore Chattanooga's deep musical heritage; the jazz history here is particularly robust.

Peruse the galleries of the Bluff View Arts District. Don't miss a stop at Rembrandt's Cafe for a coffee and pastry on the patio.

 Stay sustainable at the Crash Pad, an ecofriendly hostel in the heart of the city and the perfect base for all your outdoor adventures.

Snag an elevated charcuterie for lunch at Main Street Meats and pair it with excellent chef-selected wine – owner Erik Neil has been recognized by the James Beard Foundation multiple times, so you can't go wrong.

 Go wildlife watching at the Reflection Riding Arboretum and Nature Center – if you're lucky, you might see red-tailed hawks, bobcats and even red wolves.

Knoxville Tennessee

OUTDOOR ADVENTURES AND ARTISAN CRAFTS IN THE GATEWAY TO THE SMOKY MOUNTAINS

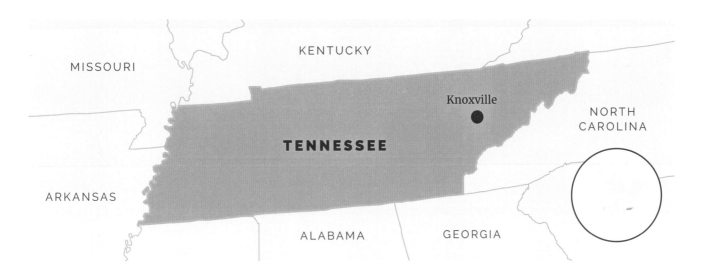

KENTUCKY

MISSOURI

Knoxville

TENNESSEE

NORTH CAROLINA

ARKANSAS

ALABAMA   GEORGIA

Over the past century, journalists haven't exactly been kind to Knoxville, referring to it as in one particularly gnarly anecdote, 'the ugliest city I ever saw.' Those words stoked a rebellious fire among Knoxvillians, who, in the 1980s, launched beautification efforts that included planting thousands of trees and reinvesting in the area's rich history and architecture.

Today, the town is a bucolic charmer, with offbeat shops, cozy restaurants, galleries and museums nestled in and around the Tennessee River. About 180 miles east of Nashville, Knoxville is the gateway to the Great Smoky Mountains and the verdant, mountainous terrain of eastern Tennessee.

Most know it as the home of the University of Tennessee, with a rabid football fan base that bleeds orange and white. But the city also plays host to one of the largest maker populations in the US, with over nine hundred artists, creatives and small-scale manufacturers transforming life around the town.

GO IF YOU LIKE...
- 🤍 *Nashville*
- 🤍 *quirky towns*
- 🤍 *rivers*
- 🤍 *college football*
- 🤍 *hiking*
- 🤍 *artisan handiwork*

Why go to Knoxville?

In Knoxville, it's easy to get a sense of Nashville before the bachelorettes took over Broadway. Or Gatlinburg before the mini-golf courses began littering the mountainous landscape. One of Knoxville's biggest draws is its proximity to the mountains and a bounty of outdoor adventures: mountain biking, paddling down the Tennessee River and exploring the Ijams Nature Center – a 318-acre natural park with 12 miles of trails, outdoor rock climbing and swimming holes in the former marble quarries that once earned Knoxville the nickname Marble City.

The city also served as the site of the last successful World's Fair held in the US. The Sunsphere – one of the only remnants of the 1982 event – still stands and houses a museum commemorating the occasion. Add in a white-hot restaurant scene and a solid dash of that infamous southern hospitality and you have an irresistible combo that warrants a repeat visit.

FIRST-TIME TIPS

Knoxville's food scene is on the rise and attracts plenty of local attention. It's wise to make reservations for dining experiences <u>a few weeks before arrival</u>.

Sporting events are a big part of life in Knoxville. The city swells with buzzy Big Orange fans on UT game days, and that can make getting around town a bit of a headache. <u>Check the game day schedule</u> prior to booking a trip.

Take advantage of Knoxville's proximity to the <u>Great Smoky Mountains National Park</u> and set aside a day to go hiking, fishing, horseback riding or wildlife watching along its many trails.

AMAZING CROWD-FREE EXPERIENCES

 Visit the World's Fair Park and take in 360-degree views of Knoxville atop the Sunsphere, the last relic of the 1982 World's Fair.

 Visit the makers in Old Town with stops at shops like Honeymouth for handmade leather goods and Pretentious Glass and Beer for glass-blowing demonstrations and pints of brew.

 Swim in a former marble quarry at the Ijams Nature Center. The sparkling blue water offers opportunities for kayaking and stand-up paddleboarding.

 Go mountain biking in south Knoxville along the Urban Wilderness Trail system, which spans 50 miles of natural surfaces fit for all skill levels.

 Paddle downstream on the Tennessee River and get a view of the University of Tennessee campus, the Vol Navy marina and botanical gardens.

 Take part in a proper tea service in the ornate Drawing Room of the Tennessean Hotel, a home away from home for visiting musicians, performers and politicians.

Above: Cheerleaders and a marching band hype up the crowd before a college football game in Neyland Stadium

GETTING THERE

McGhee Tyson is Knoxville's small commercial airport with nonstop flights to and from 28 destinations around the US. For those traveling from cities without a direct connection, Nashville and Atlanta are the next best options, offering a broader range of flight days and times. Knoxville is three hours from Nashville via rental car; Atlanta is four hours.

WHEN TO GO

Mar – Jun & late Sep – mid-Nov

Knoxville hits its stride March through June, when the iconic dogwood trails are in full bloom and temperate climes invite all manner of outdoor adventures. Fall-foliage chasers will get the most bang for their technicolor buck starting late September.

Alabama

OUTDOOR ADVENTURES IN AN UNLIKELY DESTINATION

From its northernmost cities near the Tennessee border to its southernmost tip that extends into the Gulf of Mexico, Alabama contains a plethora of natural sights. The state's many caves are of particular note and are as diverse as its ecosystems. Some are easy to explore, while others require permits and special caving equipment. But no matter what, they're always inexpensive, and a spelunking adventure can be easily combined with a long weekend getaway that takes in a tour of the Deep South.

GO IF YOU LIKE...
- 🖤 *outdoor adventures*
- 🖤 *spelunking*
- 🖤 *Mammoth Cave*
- 🖤 *Carlsbad Caverns*
- 🖤 *US history*
- 🖤 *national parks*

Alabama is well-known for its historical ties to the Civil War and the Civil Rights movement, but the state offers so much more than historical commentary: it's also one of the most biologically diverse regions in the country. Unlike its neighbors, Alabama has no major league sports teams to follow, nor does it have any popular amusement parks. Instead, it offers simplicity and natural splendor in spades. For those looking to escape the concrete jungle, a trip to Alabama's little-known underground wonders may be in order.

Why go to Alabama?

Alabama doesn't have a lot of well-known attractions, and this is why it's often overlooked. But what it lacks in top-billet sights it makes up for with its subterranean wonders. There are an astounding 4800 known caves in the state, and Jackson County, in the northeast corner, has the most caves per square mile in the entire US. When you combine these numbers with the paucity of visitors, what you get is an intimate and unique experience.

Compare some of Alabama's caves with the other big-ticket caves in North America, like Mammoth Caves and Carlsbad Caverns. Alabama's biggest cave, Majestic Caverns, only sees 100,000 visitors per year. Kentucky's Mammoth Cave, meanwhile, receives an average of 2 million visitors per year. Likewise, Sauta Cave, famous for its bat migrations, only draws 5000 visitors a year, while a similar phenomenon in Carlsbad Caverns averages a whopping half a million tourists annually.

GETTING THERE

Alabama has three major airports: Huntsville, Birmingham and Montgomery. It's also well connected with the rest of the South – several interstates bisect Alabama, connecting it with major cities like Atlanta, Nashville and New Orleans. No matter how you get here, you'll need a car to get around.

WHEN TO GO

May – Oct

Summers in Alabama can be brutally hot, but temperatures inside the caves remain in the mid-60s year-round. Summer brings longer days and the chance to see bat migrations.

Right: The mouth of a small grotto at Russell Cave National Monument.
Opposite: Flowstones and stalactites in Rickwood Caverns

FIRST-TIME TIPS

Check the websites for state and national parks as well as for privately owned caves. Websites are the best way to stay up-to-date on closures, get any required permits or sign up for a guided tour.

....

Majestic Caverns, Rickwood Caverns and Cathedral Caverns are all located within driving distance of amenities or have them on site. Sauta Cave Wildlife Reserve, Manitou Cave and Stephens Gap Callahan Cave are more rural and may not have dining or restrooms nearby.

....

Lodging around the caves can fill up during the summer months. *Advance recommendations are recommended*.

AMALING CROWD-FREE EXPERIENCES

 Marvel at the dismals in Dismals Canyon. They're often called glow worms, even though they're actually the larval stage of a unique insect. Night tours take place throughout the year.

 Take the family to DeSoto Caverns. Not only is the cavern an incredible sight, the surrounding area has kids' activities, educational talks and seasonal events.

 Swim at Rickwood Caverns State Park, where an Olympic-sized swimming pool is fed by waters direct from the cave.

 Snap photos at Stephens Gap Callahan Cave. The 143-foot pit inside the cave has a beautiful entrance and is one of the most photographed caves in North America.

 Study Native American inscriptions at Manitou Cave. This cave contains inscriptions from the Cherokee Nation on a fifty-foot-high ceiling, written over two hundred years ago.

 Delve into the past at Russell Cave National Monument. Archaeologists have uncovered artifacts representing over ten thousand years of human history here.

Roanoke Virginia

MOUNTAIN ADVENTURE HUB WITH A BURGEONING DINING SCENE

What separates Roanoke's Mill Mountain from all the others? The Mill Mountain Star, a neon star soaring eight stories above its woodsy perch overlooking downtown. Illuminated nightly, this bright beacon inspired the city's nickname: the Star City.

A former railroad town grown a bit sleepy, Roanoke emerged over the last decade as a dynamic hub for outdoor adventure – and it's easy to see why. The Blue Ridge Mountains hug the city and the Blue Ridge Parkway and Appalachian Trail are a short drive away. Cyclists use the extensive greenway system for commuting and recreation alike. Mountain biking and gravel riding are exploding thanks to the many forest roads crisscrossing the George Washington

and Jefferson National Forests and the trails tearing across Carvins Cove, the nation's second-largest urban park. Community-minded hotels, restaurants and breweries – plus a bike shop with a bar – have opened in response. It's reminiscent of Asheville, but without the lines and expensive hotels.

GO IF YOU LIKE...
- *Asheville*
- *Knoxville*
- *Chattanooga*
- *mountain biking*
- *hiking*
- *craft beer*

233

Why go to Roanoke?

A refreshing entrepreneurial spirit is sweeping this long-staid Virginia city. Located downtown, the new Fire Station One is a unique but winning combo: a furniture showroom with a boutique inn all housed in a century-old firehouse. Its Nordic-themed Stock Cafe serves up Danish smørrebrød. The nearby Liberty Trust has flipped a former bank headquarters into a stylish 54-room hotel. Even the Hotel Roanoke, a genteel stalwart, went a little steampunk with its revamped Lobby Bar. A trio of watering holes – Big Lick Brewery, Golden Cactus and Tuco's Taqueria Garaje – draw happy hour crowds to the emerging West Station while Cardinal Bike has transformed a grocery store into a bike shop, bar and coffeehouse. From there you can pedal onto the greenways and into the mountains. There's even some action in upper-crusty South Roanoke, with the invading hoi polloi creating a lively al fresco scene on Crystal Spring Ave. And SoRo seems to like it.

GETTING THERE

The primary interstate passing Roanoke is I-81, running north–south through the western edge of the state. The Blue Ridge Parkway runs parallel to I-81, but is much slower going. Roanoke is served by Amtrak, with daily service linking it to Charlottesville, Washington, DC, and New York City. The closest airport is Roanoke–Blacksburg Regional Airport.

WHEN TO GO

May – Oct

Wildflowers are blooming and waterfalls are in full force in the nearby Blue Ridge Mountains in spring. June is particularly pleasant for hiking and biking. Fall foliage blazes across the Blue Ridge in October.

FIRST-TIME TIPS

Hike McAfee Knob. This Instagram-worthy rock ledge on the Appalachian Trail draws crowds, so arrive at the trailhead parking lot as early as possible. Better yet, ride the McAfee Knob Trailhead Shuttle ($10 roundtrip) from I-81.

....

Learn the lingo before you order at the iconic 10-stool Texas Tavern diner downtown. To get you started: a cheesy is short for cheesy western, a burger topped with American cheese and an egg.

....

The 469-mile Blue Ridge Parkway links Shenandoah National Park in Virginia with Great Smoky Mountains National Park in North Carolina. Exit the parkway at mile marker 120 to reach downtown Roanoke.

Opposite, left: Cycling mixed pine forests in Carvins Cove; right: rock climbing in the Blue Ridge Mountain. Above: Roanoke has the world's largest freestanding illuminated star

AMAZING CROWD-FREE EXPERIENCES

 Check out atmospheric photographs that showcase the last years of N&W steam trains at the O Winston Link Museum.

 Spend an afternoon tubing down – or biking along – the Roanoke River in Wasena, an emerging neighborhood beside the Roanoke River Greenway that's home to fun pubs, a shave ice shop and a coffee shop. Rent tubes, kayaks and bikes at Roanoke Mountain Adventures.

 Check out an indie movie at the classic Grandin Theater, where beer and wine can accompany your popcorn and candy.

 Hike, bike or drive up Mill Mountain to its neon star, where a viewing platform provides a bird's-eye view of downtown Roanoke and beyond.

 Stroll downtown Roanoke, home to a farmers market, several museums, topnotch restaurants and numerous mom-and-pop retailers.

 Drive the Blue Ridge Parkway from Roanoke north to the Peaks of Otter, where you can hike to the summit of Sharp Top and its spectacular 360-degree views of the mountains.

Beaufort North Carolina

SMALL-TOWN CHARMER WITH SEAFOOD, QUIET BEACHES AND MARITIME HISTORY

KENTUCKY

VIRGINIA

TENNESSEE

NORTH CAROLINA

Beaufort

SOUTH CAROLINA

South of North Carolina's celebrated Outer Banks barrier islands, amid an 85-mile stretch of Atlantic coastline known as the Crystal Coast, Beaufort offers a relaxed antidote to the Southeast's better-known, and at times rowdier, beach spots. Established in the early 1700s, almost a century before North Carolina became a state, the town has a rich and complex maritime past. It's visible on the placards dotted around the storied streets of the Beaufort Historic Site, as well as in the artifacts from the shipwreck of the legendary pirate Blackbeard in the North Carolina Maritime Museum on Front Street. You'll also see it in the subtle Bahamian and Jamaican touches in the architecture of the town's mansions, built by sea captains after they returned from far-flung lands. As these influences suggest, Beaufort's seafaring history has a darker side, which it doesn't shy away from, and several locations in the town were recently designated as Sites of Memory by the Unesco Routes of Enslaved Peoples Project.

GO IF YOU LIKE...
- 💜 *seaside towns*
- 💜 *maritime history*
- 💜 *fresh seafood*
- 💜 *pirate legends*
- 💜 *US history*
- 💜 *quiet beaches*

Why go to Beaufort?

North Carolina has its fair share of laid-back coastal towns, but Beaufort is more than just another beachy bolt-hole. Its maritime heritage, small-town charm and intriguing historic district make it a unique destination, and foodies will find plenty to love in its restaurants, which range from elegant seafood eateries to welcoming down-home joints serving Carolina-style BBQ. But Beaufort is also an ideal jumping-off point for discovering another side of the Atlantic coastline. It's quieter, wilder and often accessible only by boat, a place where salt marshes melt into rolling surf on deserted islands, dolphins and turtles play in quiet estuaries and wild horses gallop along empty beaches. The Intracoastal Waterway is right on Beaufort's doorstep, making it easy to explore the nearby islands, as well as the coastal towns to the north and south. Experienced sailors may prefer to go solo, but there are plenty of guided tour options, too.

GETTING THERE

Raleigh-Durham International Airport is a three-hour drive, but the most stylish way to arrive in Beaufort is by boat, via the Intracoastal Waterway. For determined landlubbers, the Amtrak Thruway bus runs from Greenville and New Bern (North Carolina) to Morehead City, 5 miles from Beaufort.

WHEN TO GO

Apr – May, Sep – Oct

High summer is hot and humid, so for cooler temperatures and quieter vibes, plan your trip for late spring or early autumn. Although winters are chilly, there are often bright, sunny days even in December and January.

AMAZING CROWD-FREE EXPERIENCES

 Sail or take a ferry to Shackleford Banks, a barrier island known for its colony of wild horses.

 Hike over salt marshes to Fort Macon State Park, a beach and historic site set around a pre–Civil War fort.

 Kayak to the Rachel Carson Reserve, home to over two hundred species of birds, keeping your eyes peeled for dolphins and sea turtles as you paddle through the estuary.

 Soak up history and spooky vibes at Beaufort Historic Site Old Burying Ground, where majestic live oaks shade tombstones dating back as far as 1700.

 Glide 2.5 miles down the Intracoastal Waterway to Morehead City, where you can stroll the boardwalk before enjoying fresh seafood at a waterfront restaurant.

 Hop on a ferry to Sand Dollar Island, where adults and kids alike will enjoy snorkeling in shallow tide pools and beachcombing for sand dollars and shells.

Clockwise from left: Wild horses roam the coast; old burial ground in Roanoke; pre-Civil War relics at Fort Macon State Park

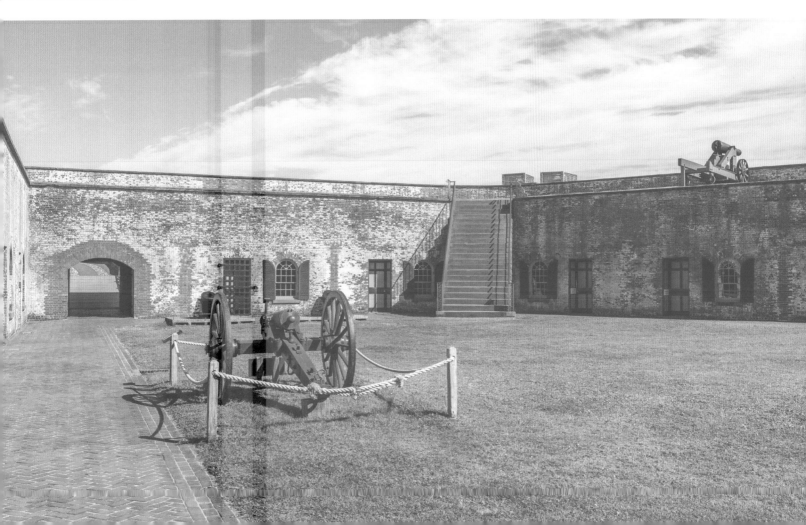

Opposite: The hypnotic spiral of Finlay Park Fountain

Columbia South Carolina

RIVER ADVENTURES AND A REVITALIZED DOWNTOWN ENERGIZE THIS FRIENDLY TOWN

Take the culinary and cultural offerings. Yes, you'll find scads of restaurants dishing out South Carolina specialties like shrimp and grits and pimento cheese, a popular cheese-and-mayo spread, but you're as likely to hear passionate recommendations for Korean and Lebanese restaurants and a vegan soul-food joint. Art galleries and museum exhibitions are edgy and immersive while festivals embrace an array of offbeat themes. It all feels energized, entrepreneurial and fun. Outdoor adventures converge on the Saluda and Congaree Rivers, which propel inner tubes and kayaks through the thick of the city.

GO IF YOU LIKE...
- 🤍 *Austin*
- 🤍 *Nashville*
- 🤍 *national parks*
- 🤍 *river fun*
- 🤍 *college towns*
- 🤍 *vibrant dining scene*

Flanked by a river, anchored by a statehouse and home to a beloved state university, Columbia has a lot in common with Austin, Texas. But the vibe? These days Columbia, nicknamed Cola by locals, evokes Austin from 20 years ago, when the latter was keeping it weird and didn't have traffic problems. Although Columbia is more friendly than weird – this is South Carolina, y'all – there is a feisty can-do energy here that's refreshing and unexpected.

Why go to Columbia?

Thanks to the opening of a 20-story student housing complex in 2014, downtown's Main Street is busy well into the night, no longer shuttering after the workday. New restaurants and coffee shops have sprung up in support while old favorites have found new life. The Soda City Market, held every Saturday along a four-block stretch of Main, welcomes 150 vendors while the 40-year-old Nickelodeon, dubbed the Nick, screens indie films and hosts cutting-edge film series. Opening in 2023, the Our Story Matters gallery at the Columbia Museum of Art spotlights Black history in the city. Decor in two new hotels, the boutique Hotel Trundle and the college-themed Graduate Columbia, gives a loving nod to the state. Segra Park, which opened in 2016 in the emerging Bull Street District, hosts the minor league Columbia Fireflies, named for the synchronous fireflies that illuminate Congaree National Park every May.

GETTING THERE

Columbia sits in the center of South Carolina at the junction of three interstates: I-20, I-26 and I-77. The city is a convenient stop between Charleston, SC, about two hours southeast, and Asheville, NC, about 2½ hours northwest. Columbia Metropolitan Airport (CAE) is seven miles from downtown. Amtrak's Silver Service/Palmetto line between Miami and New York City stops in Columbia daily.

WHEN TO GO

Mar – Oct

If temperature is your deciding factor, visit in spring or fall when the weather is pleasant; avoid the hot and muggy summer months. If steamy temps don't bother you, come for festivals and river fun in summer.

AMAZING CROWD-FREE EXPERIENCES

 Swoop over the Lower Saluda River on a 1000-foot-long zipline at the Riverbanks Zoo and Garden, home to more than three thousand animals and a new aquarium and reptile center.

 Explore old-growth hardwood forest at Congaree National Park on the Boardwalk Trail, or paddle past moss-draped trees on the Cedar Creek Canoe Trail.

 Bike the paved, ADA-accessible Three Rivers Greenway as it ribbons alongside the Congaree, Saluda and Broad Rivers for more than 15 miles.

 Inner tube down the Lower Saluda to the Congaree River, then enjoy a German-style craft beer at Bierkeller Brewing Company's new digs beside the Congaree.

 Learn about the Reconstruction era and its African American trailblazers in Columbia on the self-guided Reconstructed tour through the Historic District.

 Check out the Busted Plug, one of many eye-catching public art pieces across the city, and then explore The Vista, the city's arts and culture district.

Opposite, top: The African American History Monument; **bottom**: swamps and cypress trees at Congaree National Park

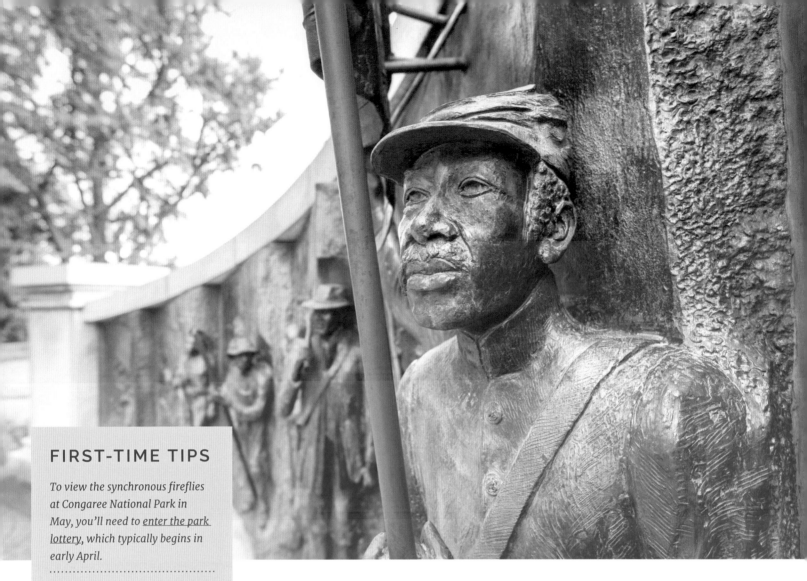

FIRST-TIME TIPS

To view the synchronous fireflies at Congaree National Park in May, you'll need to <u>enter the park lottery</u>, which typically begins in early April.

· ·

If you're visiting in summer and want some lazy fun in the water, <u>rent an inner tube from Palmetto Outdoors</u> – they'll shuttle you to the starting point. Bring cash.

· ·

Pimento cheese really is a thing here. To get started, download the <u>Pimento Cheese Passport</u> (experiencecolumbiasc.com), which lists more than a dozen restaurants serving delicious pimento cheese dishes.

· ·

Word of warning: Columbia, like Austin, is <u>ferociously hot</u> in summer.

Opposite: Turrets capping the defensive walls of Castillo de San Marcos fort

St Augustine Florida

SUSTAINABLE SAILING AND LOCAVORE DINING IN A CHARMING OLD-WORLD SETTLEMENT

It's hard not to see glimmers of the old world among St Augustine's narrow cobbled streets and centuries-old Spanish and British architecture. Henry Flagler harnessed that beauty when he fashioned the city into a luxury destination for his wealthy acquaintances in the late 1800s, and it's a vision that's endured ever since.

Located a little over one hundred miles from Orlando, the city and its surrounding neighborhoods are full of family-friendly activities. Families can explore the wooden mazes and forts on the Project Swing playground, watch reenactments of early colonial life in the Historic District, comb the shore for seashells and stop in the heaps of ice cream shops around town.

But adults will also find plenty to hold their attention, whether it be in a hand-crafted cocktail made in a former ice plant or listening to live music on St George Street. St Augustine is a city that adapts to the currents of time – and to the people who call on its company.

GO IF YOU LIKE...
💜 *Europe*
💜 *history*
💜 *beaches*
💜 *sailing*
💜 *farmers markets*
💜 *family travel*

Why go to St Augustine?

Founded in 1565 by the Spanish, St Augustine is the oldest continuously occupied European settlement in the US. A focus on locally sourced dining and sustainability efforts touch on everything from its sparkling waterways to the farmers market held under towering oaks.

Starting with the fresh seafood plucked out of the waters of Salt Run and Matanzas Bay to the datil peppers and the potatoes that thrive in the region, chefs are exploring the area's bounty and making it the focus of their menus. Dining hot spots like the Floridian, Forgotten Tonic, Catch 27 and Ancient City Brunch Bar are just a handful of rising stars harnessing the region's natural resources.

The city also has a renewed commitment to preserving its history – and its future. Boaters and marine biologists are protecting the area's waterways through consumer education, while the Green Hands Initiative works to reduce the ecological footprint of live events.

GETTING THERE

Accessing St Augustine will require a car. The city is a 50-minute drive from Jacksonville International Airport. You'll find more flight options and flexibility at Orlando International Airport, which is a 90-minute drive to St Augustine.

WHEN TO GO

Nov – Apr

Hurricane season ends in late November, ushering in a period of lower humidity, drier weather and lower daytime temps. January through March is peak season, when snowbirds descend from the frigid northern states.

FIRST-TIME TIPS

Watch the <u>weather forecast</u> for summer trips – hurricane season runs from June to November, and storm activity peaks in late August and September.

<u>Make reservations</u> for meals and tours at least a week or two before you arrive. Popular restaurants and attractions fill up fast.

<u>Parking is notoriously difficult</u> in St Augustine, especially near the Historic District. Leave your car in the Historic Downtown Parking Facility and explore on foot or trolley.

Exploring the <u>Historic District</u> with its quirky shops and attractions is a must, but go during the week. The narrow streets can get crowded on weekends.

AMAZING CROWD-FREE EXPERIENCES

 Spot a pod of dolphins from a sailboat while learning about marine life and local conservation efforts through St Augustine Sailing's Science Adventures.

 Climb to the top of the St Augustine Lighthouse, on Anastasia Island that's over 145 years old.

 Head to the Farmers Market on Saturday morning and pick up jars of honey infused with the local datil pepper.

 Sample locally crafted spirits during the free tour at the St Augustine Distillery, a decade-old operation that mills, distills and bottles its spirits by hand.

 Stroll among rare and endangered palms, live oaks and 2400 species of plants at St John's Botanical Garden and Nature Preserve in Hastings, a 30-minute drive from St Augustine.

 Go hunting for fossilized shark teeth when it's low tide on the shores of Vilano Beach.

Clockwise from top left: Plaza de la Constitución; arts and crafts on St George Street; a roseate spoonbill takes to the air

Hollywood Florida

STREET ART AND FAMILY ADVENTURES BREATHE NEW LIFE INTO AN OLD BEACH TOWN

SOUTH CAROLINA

GEORGIA

FLORIDA

Hollywood

Miami and Fort Lauderdale steal most of South Florida's sun-drenched spotlight, but nestled between the two behemoths lies a funky little beach town. Hollywood (no, not that Hollywood) charmingly straddles old Florida coastal life with edgy food, art and architecture trickling down from its bigger siblings to the north and south.

Located 20 miles north of Miami, Hollywood draws about five million visitors a year – a modest sum compared to Miami's 26.5 million. But those who stop here will revel in the turquoise waters, amber shores and the iconic Broadwalk without the crush of human bodies and the cacophony found on South Beach.

Just blocks from the beach you'll find a vibrant street art scene pushing itself up through the modern nooks and crannies constructed around the city's cultural heart: Young Circle, where families regularly gather for movie nights, live concerts and laconic afternoons spent under shade trees or cooling off on the resident splash pad.

GO IF YOU LIKE...
- *Miami*
- *Fort Lauderdale*
- *small beach towns*
- *water sports*
- *street art*
- *family activities*

Why go to Hollywood?

The trappings of mass development and frenetic urban hustle seem to have quietly bypassed Hollywood's shores. Meandering down the Broadwalk and dipping into the shops around downtown can feel like another time and place, one that harkens back to slower pleasures: listening to live music at dusk on a park lawn, leisurely strolling in the sand as the sun rises off the coast or enjoying an old-fashioned sundae from Jaxson's Ice Cream Parlor, a local institution that's been dishing up treats for nearly 70 years. And that can be a welcome respite from the relentless energy pulsating from Miami and Fort Lauderdale.

But when you're ready to ramp up the energy, Hollywood can turn up the volume without overwhelming the senses. Nearby, both the Seminole Hard Rock Hotel and Casino and the Diplomat Beach Resort offer lively pool scenes, buzzy restaurants and pulsating nightlife options that keep things from getting too staid.

FIRST-TIME TIPS

Dive into the area's art scene with the Downtown Hollywood Art Walk *held every third Thursday of the month. Count on a free evening of gallery tours and live music.*

....

Keep tabs on the weather in the summer – hurricane season *runs from June to November, but storm activity really picks in August and September and can potentially upend plans with airport and road closures.*

....

Check the schedule for ArtsPark at Young Circle *before you arrive – there's typically a family movie night every Friday, but live acts also make their way to the outdoor stage.*

AMAZING CROWD-FREE EXPERIENCES

 Rent a bike and cruise the Hollywood Beach Broadwalk taking in coastal views along the brick-paved thoroughfare.

 Learn the art of glass-blowing from the glass-making pros at Hollywood Hot Glass in Young Park and pick up some jewel-colored souvenirs to take home.

 Grab locally grown eats at the Yellow Green Farmer's Market and enjoy them under the massive tiki hut. But first, join the free yoga class offered on weekends.

 Sip local brews at 3 Sons Brewing, a kid-friendly brewery serving up unique beers (Neapolitan Ice Cream stout) from 26 different taps along with savory Neapolitan pies.

 Catch the Guitar Hotel Light Show at the Seminole Hard Rock Hotel and Casino where choreographed high-powered beams dance 20,000 feet in the sky.

 Head west to the Everglades and spend a day on an airboat skimming over the river of grass and spotting alligators, spoonbills and mangrove habitats.

Left: Pastel-colored buildings by Hollywood Beach; **below**: the Seminole Hard Rock Hotel crowned with a giant guitar

GETTING THERE

Hollywood is conveniently close to Fort Lauderdale–Hollywood International Airport. The 8-mile journey only takes around 20 minutes via taxi, rideshare or rental car. While the quickest way to access Hollywood is from this airport, Miami International Airport offers exponentially more flight options. Getting to Hollywood from Miami can take anywhere from 40 minutes to over an hour.

WHEN TO GO

Nov – Apr

Hurricane season ends in late November, ushering in a period of lower humidity and temps during the day. January through March is peak season for the area; snowbirds start returning north as summer approaches.

This spread:
Spruce Head Island, Maine

Northeast
USA

Opposite: Bucks County's theater scene thrives inside a restored mill

Bucks County Pennsylvania

RIVETING HISTORY, RELAXING GREEN SPACES AND AN ARTISTIC LEGACY

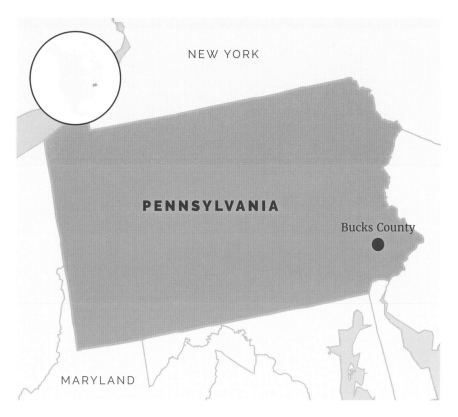

NEW YORK

PENNSYLVANIA

Bucks County

MARYLAND

a fated Christmas crossing during the Revolutionary War. The region was part of the Underground Railroad in the 18th and 19th centuries. And before that, the Lenni Lenape were the land's first inhabitants before they were forced to relocate in the 1860s.

Beyond its history, explore the region's charming boutique- and gallery-lined main streets in towns like New Hope, Doylestown and Newtown, as well as the miles of hiking and biking trails that run along the river and through sprawling parks and woodlands.

GO IF YOU LIKE...
- 🖤 *small towns*
- 🖤 *American history*
- 🖤 *antiquing*
- 🖤 *art galleries*
- 🖤 *bird-watching*
- 🖤 *LBGTIQ+ history*

Abucolic patchwork of farmland, orchards and state parks, Bucks County feels much more remote than its location just 25 miles north of Philadelphia's Center City. It's one of Philly's five counties, and one of the original three envisioned by city founder William Penn. While history buffs flock to Philadelphia to explore the origins of American democracy, Bucks County, a hop, skip and a jump up the Delaware River, offers plenty of its own compelling history. George Washington traversed the same river with his Continental Army on

Why go to Bucks County?

In addition to acres of public green space, the region is home to a rich cultural legacy that's inspired generations of artists, actors and writers. Visitors can get a sense of it at the Michener Art Museum, which houses an expansive collection, including the works of Pennsylvania Impressionists. The Pearl S Buck house is the former estate of the Nobel prize–winning writer and is now a National Historic Landmark. Ceramicist Henry Chapman Mercer amassed a vast collection of pieces inspired by the American arts and crafts movement, now on display at the Mercer Museum and Fonthill Castle.

New Hope makes for a prime jumping-off point. Accommodations like the Ghost Light Inn and the River House at Odette's offer a fresh take on the region's historic bed and breakfasts. Nearby is Bowman's Wildflower Preserve, particularly beautiful in spring, and the Delaware Canal State Park, with a 77-mile trail that runs along the historic towpath.

GETTING THERE

From Philadelphia, Septa public buses run to towns throughout Bucks County, but the best way to travel is by car. Take I-95 from anywhere on the East Coast (75 miles from New York City and 150 miles from Washington, DC) and I-276 (the Pennsylvania Turnpike) coming from the west.

WHEN TO GO

Sep – Nov

Bucks County has year-round appeal, but the brilliant fall foliage is an especially compelling backdrop for hiking, bird-watching and scenic drives. It's also harvest season, so visitors can enjoy an array of local produce, including apples and pumpkins.

AMAZING CROWD-FREE EXPERIENCES

 Bring a hammer to Ringing Rocks County Park, where you can hike across the seven-acre field of iron-rich volcanic boulders that, when struck, make a distinctive chime.

 Watch history unfold at Washington Crossing Historic Park during a Christmas day reenactment of the general leading his troops across the Delaware River.

 Admire the outdoor sculptures and American Impressionist works at the Michener Art Museum in Doylestown, or pop into indie art galleries on Bridge Street in New Hope.

 In the fall, pick your own apples at Solebury Orchards, and come back in the summer to harvest blueberries, cherries and fresh-cut flowers.

 On a hot day, float down the Delaware River. Rent a tube with Bucks County River Country and take in the surrounding woodlands from the water.

 Keep your eyes peeled for red-tailed hawks, osprey and bald eagles at the Peace Valley Nature Center, a designated Important Bird Area with miles of paved trails, ponds and streams.

Opposite top: Picking apples at Solebury Orchards in New Hope; **bottom**: Fonthill Castle has dozens of ornate rooms

FIRST-TIME TIPS

Embark on a _self-guided driving tour_ of the area's 12 covered bridges, a distinct architectural calling card of the region.

Stay the night at the _Ghost Light Inn_, a riverfront boutique hotel that's walking distance to New Hope's restaurants and art galleries.

See a show at the historic _Bucks County Playhouse_. Since its opening in 1939, legends from Harpo Marx to Robert Redford have graced the venue's stage.

New Hope has long been a welcoming enclave for the _LGBTIQ+ community_. If you visit in June, don't miss the annual Pride parades here, as well as in Doylestown and Perkasie.

Assateague Island National Seashore Maryland

UNWIND ON THE BEACHES AND TRAILS SURROUNDED BY WILD HORSES

PENNSYLVANIA

MARYLAND

DELAWARE

WEST VIRGINIA

VIRGINIA

Assateague Island
National Seashore

According to local lore, Assateague Island's most famous residents are the descendants of a band of horses that survived an 18th-century Spanish shipwreck. But according to the National Park Service, the more likely explanation is that farmers brought their horses here to graze in the 17th century in order to avoid having to pay taxes on them.

However they got here, the wild horses are the main draw on Assateague, a 37-mile barrier island off the coast of Maryland and Virginia. In Maryland, you'll see horses wandering the dunes and grazing by the side of the road — don't be surprised if a crossing horse holds up traffic. In Virginia, where the horses are privately owned by the Chincoteague fire department and fenced in, you can watch them from an observation platform on the Woodland Trail and in the marshes along Beach Road.

But the horses are just part of the draw. Travelers also come here for the unspoiled beaches, hiking and biking trails and campsites near the waves.

GO IF YOU LIKE...
- *Ocean City*
- *wild horses*
- *gentle hikes*
- *camping*
- *bird-watching*
- *beaches*

Why go to Assateague Island National Seashore?

Assateague offers a unique landscape that changes with the tide – it's essentially a constantly moving sand bar – making it an experience worth visiting time and again. On the Maryland side, there are two main areas: the 2-mile Assateague State Park, located at the north entrance to the island, and the Assateague Island National Seashore, which comprises everything else.

The Virginia portion of Assateague Island contains the Chincoteague National Wildlife Refuge, whose forests, beaches and marshes protect migratory plants and birds. Altogether, the island receives 2.5 million visitors annually, but most arrive in summer. While that might seem like a lot, it's only a fraction of the annual visitors to ever-popular Ocean City, the closest town to Assateague in Maryland. Hiking trails run from the family-friendly and wheelchair-accessible Life of the Marsh Trail (.5 mile) to the longer Service Road (7.5 miles), where hikers might see waterfowl, deer and rabbits.

GETTING THERE

There are three major airports in the Baltimore–Washington metro area; Baltimore/Washington International (BWI) is the closest to Assateague, and is roughly 2½ hours from the Maryland entrance. The Virgina entrance is about a three-hour drive. While most visitors arrive by car, cyclists and pedestrians in Maryland can use a dedicated path to enter Assateague Island free of charge.

WHEN TO GO

Sep & Oct

Autumn is ideal: the water remains warm enough to hit the beach, but kids are back in school and the crowds have tapered off.

FIRST-TIME TIPS

There are no gas stations, shops or restaurants here; fuel the car and your belly before arriving.

....

There's virtually no shade, so bring an umbrella or hat during the summer and wear sunscreen. Insect repellent will deter mosquitos, flies and ticks.

....

Enter from either the Maryland or Virginia side. You can't drive from one end to the other without returning to the mainland.

....

There are visitor centers on both the Maryland and Virginia sides.

....

Maintain a 40-foot distance from horses, and don't feed or touch them, as they can kick and bite.

AMAZING CROWD-FREE EXPERIENCES

Strike out into the dunes with a 4WD vehicle to get away from it all. You'll need an over-sand vehicle permit.

Rent a kayak – or bring your own – and paddle out into the Chincoteague and Sinepuxent Bays by yourself or with Assateague Explorer tours.

Pitch your tent on the sand and fall asleep to the sound of crashing waves. Reserve sites in advance and note that camping is permitted in Maryland only.

Backpack on the Maryland side of the island; you'll need to carry your own water and obtain a backcountry camping permit.

Take an ecotour with Assateague Adventures or Assateague Island Tours in the off-season to view ponies and birds from the water.

Bike or hike between the marshes and forests on the 3.25-mile paved Wildlife Loop. It's only open to pedestrians and cyclists before 3pm.

Opposite: Wild horses roam the sands of Assateague Island; **Above**: Salt marshes are a haven for birdlife

© JENINVA / SHUTTERSTOCK. © DANITA DELIMONT / SHUTTERSTOCK

Opposite: Bucktown General Store, where Harriet Tubman refused to help restrain an enslaved man

Harriet Tubman Historical Park Delaware & Maryland

EXHIBITS HIGHLIGHT THE ABOLITIONIST'S LIFE ON MARYLAND'S EASTERN SHORE

PENNSYLVANIA

MARYLAND

DELAWARE

Harriet Tubman
Historic Park

WEST
VIRGINIA

VIRGINIA

Visitors first arrive at a striking contemporary building that contrasts with the 17-acre green park and farmland surrounding it. The Maryland Department of Natural Resources and National Park Service comanage the site, made with red cedar on one side – symbolizing Harriet Tubman's time working in timber fields – and a self-repairing zinc patina on the other, signifying how Black Americans have healed themselves from the brutal legacy of slavery.

The location in Church Creek, two hours from DC, carries significance. It's midway between Tubman's birthplace in Peter's Neck, MD, and Brodess Farm in Bucktown, where her family was enslaved. A 17-minute film and multimedia exhibits highlight Tubman's childhood in Dorchester County and her

escape to freedom – a precarious journey she made an estimated 13 times to rescue as many as 70 enslaved family members and friends. The park's displays provide a detailed introduction to other sites along the Harriet Tubman Byway, a self-guided driving route with 46 stops significant to the abolitionist's life.

GO IF YOU LIKE...
- *National Museum of African American History and Culture*
- *African American heritage*
- *American history*
- *unspoiled nature*
- *bird-watching*
- *small museums*

Why go to the Harriet Tubman Historical Park?

As the United States continues to reconcile with its history of slavery, the exhibits and sites along the Harriet Tubman Byway serve as a reminder of past racial injustices. Making its debut in 2017, the state park and byway remain relatively undiscovered, receiving 43,000 visitors in 2022, the year that also marked the two hundredth anniversary of Tubman's birth.

The exhibits contain intriguing details about the abolitionist's early life. She went by Araminta 'Minty' Ross until her marriage in 1844 to John Tubman, a free man. Even after her marriage Tubman remained a slave, and it wasn't until 1849 that John Tubman used the stars to guide Harriet to Philadelphia, passing through the region's vast marshes, which have remained untouched since her time. Interactive touchscreen displays allow visitors to imagine guiding enslaved persons who faced recapture during their escapes. Bird-watchers can get their fill of nature while traversing the same landscape that Tubman once did.

GETTING THERE

Visitors can take the county public bus from Rte 50 to downtown Cambridge, where you'll find a few noteworthy Tubman sites. Most visitors from DC (two hours) or Philadelphia (2½ hours) will travel Rte 50 by car to get to the national park and sites along the byway.

WHEN TO GO

Sep & Oct

Visiting during the fall allows guests to enjoy the many outdoor attractions and special events, while avoiding the brutal summer heat.

FIRST-TIME TIPS

The _Dorchester Visitor Center_ should be your first stop in a scenic waterfront park. Pick up an area map with sites on the byway.

Check the _park program schedule_ to hear rangers share stories about other lesser-known abolitionists.

Kids can pick up a _junior ranger activity booklet_ and get a badge upon completion.

Most _accommodation options_ on the southern part of the byway are located in Cambridge, Maryland.

If you're visiting during International Underground Railroad Month in September, stay for the park's _Emancipation Day_ celebration with kids' games and a Harriet Tubman reenactor.

Left: A rare carte de visite portrait of Harriet Tubman; **right**: signs point out important locations from her life. **Opposite**: The 13 foot bronze Beacon of Hope statue

HARRIET TUBMAN
BORN ARAMINTA ROSS 1822

AMAZING CROWD-FREE EXPERIENCES

 Spot muskrats, river otters and geese at the Blackwater National Wildlife Refuge, whose waterways once protected Tubman.

 Break out the binoculars to view blue herons, bald eagles and other migratory birds at the Hyatt Chesapeake Bay's 18-acre Blue Heron Rookery, open August to Dec 15.

 Visit downtown Cambridge to explore the walkable sites along the Harriet Tubman Byway, including the Dorchester County Courthouse with its 13-foot bronze Beacon of Hope statue of Tubman.

 Engage with the exhibits and programs at the Harriet Tubman Museum and Education Center in downtown Cambridge. The striking *Take My Hand* mural on the outside features Tubman's outstretched hand welcoming visitors inside.

 Make an appointment to go inside the Bucktown General Store, where a defiant Tubman was hit by an iron weight, which led to epileptic seizures throughout her life.

 Stop at Harriet Tubman's childhood home at Brodess Farm, where she lived with her parents, eight siblings and their enslaver Edward Brodess.

The Brandywine Valley Delaware

HISTORIC ESTATES AND INSPIRED GARDENS IN DELAWARE'S CHATEAU COUNTRY

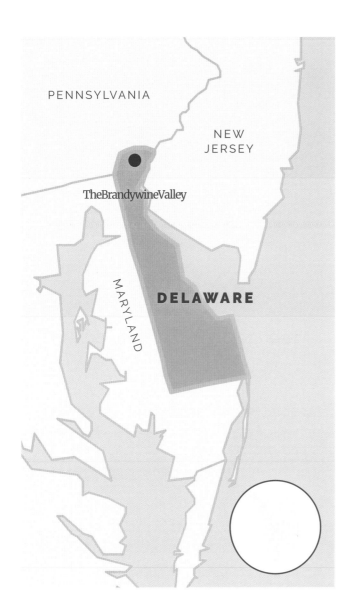

PENNSYLVANIA

NEW JERSEY

The Brandywine Valley

MARYLAND

DELAWARE

Just outside Wilmington's well-traversed highways is the Brandywine Valley. Straddling Delaware's northern border and the southeastern corner of Pennsylvania, the valley is home to such a rich trove of ancestral estates, gardens and cultural gems that it's known colloquially as Chateau Country.

At the turn of the 19th century, Pierre–Samuel du Pont de Nemours fled the French Revolution and emigrated to the region with his two sons. The younger, Éleuthère, founded a gunpowder manufacturing company in 1802 on the banks of the Brandywine River. The powder mill is now part of Hagley Museum, an enduring symbol of du Pont innovation, while family homes like Nemours Estate and Winterthur, also open to the public, are a testament of the fortune they sparked. On the Pennsylvania side of the region, the Brandywine Museum of Art celebrates another family dynasty: the Wyeths. The works of three generations of painters – Andrew, NC and Jamie – are displayed here among a collection of other American artists.

GO IF YOU LIKE...
- *English countryside*
- *manicured gardens*
- *American art*
- *hiking*
- *Industrial Revolution history*
- *canoeing and kayaking*

Why go to the Brandywine Valley?

Among the du Pont family legacies is the Nemours Estate, a 77-room neoclassical manse built to resemble a French chateau and embellished by Versailles-inspired gardens. A few miles away, Winterthur, the one-time home of grandson Henry Francis du Pont, holds the vast collection of decorative arts he amassed throughout his life, including furniture, textiles and some 19,000 ceramic objects. The one thousand surrounding acres includes the whimsical Enchanted Woods, an essential stop for those visiting with children.

Its founder's spirit of ingenuity lives on at Hagley, an indoor-outdoor museum on the site of the company's original headquarters and powder mill. The du Pont family's legacy extends just over the Pennsylvania border in the Brandywine Valley with Longwood Gardens. The world-class botanical garden encompasses over one thousand acres of gardens, woodlands and meadows, along with a new show spotlighting the recently renovated fountains.

GETTING THERE

The Brandywine Valley is easily accessible from Philadelphia (one-hour drive) and Washington, DC (2½-hour drive), via I-95. From the Wilmington exit, state routes 52 and 100 form part of the Brandywine Valley National Scenic Byway. There's no public transportation that serves the sights.

WHEN TO GO

May – Nov

Visit in the fall for mild weather and spectacular foliage. In the summer months, riverfront activities like canoeing and kayaking are on offer, as well as plenty of outdoor festivals and concerts.

AMAZING CROWD-FREE EXPERIENCES

 Search for fairies at Winterthur's Enchanted Woods. The children's garden is part of the historic property's one thousand acres of woodlands and gardens.

 Paddle down the Brandywine River in a canoe or kayak. Northbrook Canoe Company rents boats and arranges the shuttle to the put-in, too.

 Tour the original du Pont family home and gardens at Hagley Museum, and stay for a walk along the Brandywine River.

 Pack a picnic and head to Mt Cuba Center, a seven-acre botanical garden with fewer visitors than Longwood Gardens and plenty of native plants.

 Immerse yourself in regional paintings and sculptures at the Brandywine Museum of Art, set in a former mill on the banks of the Brandywine in Chadds Ford, Pennsylvania.

 Scale Delaware's only rock-climbing crag at Alapocas Run State Park, a wooded haven with granite cliffs, native pawpaw trees and hiking trails.

Opposite: Formal gardens at the 200-acre Nemours Estate

FIRST-TIME TIPS

If you visit in May, <u>join the tailgate at Point to Point</u>, the lively steeplechase horse race.

History buffs should arrange to visit the <u>Winterthur Library</u>, which holds a staggering collection of rare books, manuscripts and photographs dating as far back as the 17th century. Reserve.

Reserve a timed admission slot for <u>Longwood Gardens</u> and visit the century-old glass conservatory first, which gets more crowded as the day goes on.

Book a room at the <u>Inn at Montchanin</u>, a boutique hotel set in a collection of restored 19th-century buildings with stone walls, fireplaces and soaking tubs.

Staten Island New York

GREEN SPACES, HISTORIC BUILDINGS AND A GLOBAL DINING SCENE

Wu-Tang Clan and Pete Davidson. Those who do disembark at St George Terminal will find homestyle food, a museum honoring lighthouses and their keepers, a restored performing arts venue and much more.

Once home to Irish and Italian immigrants, Staten Island now has a Sri Lankan community in Tompkinsville and Stapleton, and Sandy Ground is one of NYC's oldest continuously settled free Black settlements. Meanwhile, a nationally designated landmark of LGBTIQ+ history, the Alice Austen House Museum, honors this female photographer and her relationship with life partner Gertrude Tate.

Beyond the reach of the subway, Staten Island is often touted as New York City's forgotten borough. Its residents only number 496,000, but more than 22 million passengers ride the free Staten Island Ferry annually...most of them for roundtrip views of the Statue of Liberty and Ellis Island, rather than to actually visit.

But Staten Island has garnered more attention of late, both as the setting for mockudrama *What We Do in the Shadows* and because of locals like the

GO IF YOU LIKE...
- 🤍 *maritime history*
- 🤍 *cultural venues*
- 🤍 *historic architecture*
- 🤍 *pizzerias*
- 🤍 *Sri Lankan cuisine*
- 🤍 *public parks*

Why go to Staten Island?

The 'greenest borough,' Staten Island has over 170 parks and 12,300 acres of protected parkland, the equivalent of more than a third of the island. The Greenbelt is a 2800-acre system of park lands and nature preserves, its nature centers incorporating educational programming. Joining this list is Freshkills Park, a redeveloped landfill that's three times the size of Central Park and scheduled to open in phases through 2036.

Snug Harbor Cultural Center and Botanical Garden has evolved from a retired sailors home into a complex housing the Staten Island Museum, a maritime museum, a children's museum and gardens and a conservatory. A self-guided tour highlights key points of interest. There's more history at Conference House Park, where an unsuccessful Revolutionary War peace conference took place between the Americans and the British.

In 2022, the Staten Island FerryHawks brought baseball back to the borough; their home games are played at Staten Island University Hospital Community Park.

GETTING THERE

The Staten Island Ferry operates 24/7, running from the Whitehall Terminal in Lower Manhattan to St George. The NYC Ferry connects to St George from Midtown West and Battery Park City, while some MTA buses run to and from Manhattan and Brooklyn.

The Staten Island Railway is an in-borough rapid transit line. The Staten Island Expressway connects to Long Island.

WHEN TO GO

Apr – Jul & Sep – Nov

Spring and fall are good times to visit. Summers in New York City are hot and humid, but there are plenty of festivals and beaches are open. Winter is chilly, but public venues stage seasonal events.

Opposite: Towers of Battery Weed fort overlooking the Narrows. **Above, left**: The venerable Egger's Ice Cream Parlor; **right**: photographer Alice Austen's house and gallery

AMAZING CROWD-FREE EXPERIENCES

Wander along the hiking trails at Blue Heron Park while looking for owls, herons, songbirds, ospreys, turtles and the hooded merganser.

Look for the sharp-tailed sparrows, wood ducks, herons, egrets, ibis, gulls, snapping turtles and cormorants at the Greenbelt Conservancy's William T Davis Wildlife Refuge. This was the first wildlife preserve established in NYC.

Admire Tibetan Buddhist art and ritual objects at the Jacques Marchais Museum of Tibetan Art; this complex of fieldstone buildings was designed to look like a hillside Tibetan monastery.

Learn about Antonio Meucci, the inventor of the first telephone, and Italian general and political leader Giuseppe Garibaldi, at the Garibaldi-Meucci Museum.

Ride the Carousel for All Children at Willowbrook Park, which is operated seasonally and adorned with hand-carved mythical beasts, endangered species and painted renderings of Staten Island landmarks.

Visit the remains of Fort Wadsworth, one of the oldest military installations in the United States.

Ithaca New York

WATERFALLS AND GORGES TRAVERSE A MAJESTIC CAMPUS AND HISTORIC NEIGHBORHOODS

When viewed from space, central New York State looks like it's been pawed by a gargantuan bear. That's thanks to the Finger Lakes: 11 slender bodies of water that glaciers carved out two million years ago. At the southern tip of the longest lake, Cayuga – named for the region's Indigenous nation – is the Ivy League college town of Ithaca. Its unofficial slogan, 'Ithaca is Gorges,' spotlights the area's dramatic topography. Three streams tumble through forested canyons and into the town itself, which is famed for its counterculture vibe, civic activism, street festivals and lively arts scene.

Harnessed to run factories in the pre-steam era, these streams are at their most breathtaking when cascading over a series of waterfalls – including spectacular Ithaca Falls – on their way through Cornell University's campus and picturesque neighborhoods, which have remained largely unchanged for over a century.

A bit out of town is the Finger Lakes wine country, renowned for its aromatic Rieslings, whose grapes flourish in the microclimates created by Cayuga and Seneca Lakes.

GO IF YOU LIKE…
- 🤍 *Niagara Falls*
- 🤍 *forest strolls*
- 🤍 *campus vibes*
- 🤍 *chiming bells*
- 🤍 *fine wines*
- 🤍 *crisp apples*

Why go to Ithaca?

Only six square miles, Ithaca packs in a surprising array of sights and activities. After hiking along the rushing cascades of Fall Creek or Cascadilla Gorge, meander over to Collegetown to grab a bagel or dine on authentic Korean or Chinese food. For more dining options – including Moosewood Restaurant, which in 1974 helped launch the American vegetarian movement by publishing the Moosewood Cookbook – head down the hill to Ithaca's town center and its focal point, the Commons, a pedestrian precinct where you can shop for locally made crafts or, in summer, attend free outdoor concerts.

For the freshest locavore fruits and veggies, drop by the member-run Ithaca Farmers Market, open on weekends except in winter. Keen on catching an Ivy League football game, hockey match or athletics meet? Check out cornellbigred.com for tickets. Venues such as Cornell's Bailey Hall and the 1600-seat State Theatre host classical and pop concerts, jam sessions, plays, dance performances and, of course, lectures by leading international scholars.

GETTING THERE

Ithaca is roughly halfway between New York City and Toronto – it's a bit over four hours by road from each – and is linked to both cities by bus, with multiple daily runs to various locations in Manhattan. A handful of daily flights link Ithaca Tompkins International Airport with the New York City area (JFK and Newark).

WHEN TO GO

Apr – Oct

Wildflowers carpet the hillsides in spring, while summer is ideal for hiking and lazy lakeside strolls. Autumn is known for its flamboyant fall foliage. Winters tend to be cold and snowy.

AMAZING CROWD-FREE EXPERIENCES

 Roam around the Cornell campus and its 19th-century Arts Quad. Take in panoramic views from Libe Slope and stroll along Cascadilla Gorge, all to the accompaniment of the Cornell Chimes.

 Explore the Cornell Botanic Gardens. Hike among native species, walk around Beebe Lake or dip your toes in Fall Creek at Flat Rock.

 Spot wild birds at Sapsucker Woods, run by the Cornell Lab of Ornithology, and identify them with the help of Cornell's own Merlin Bird ID app.

 Enter into the fantastical world of dinosaurs at the Cornell-affiliated Museum of the Earth, with exhibits on the geological origins of the Finger Lakes.

 Walk to the base of Taughannock Falls, the highest single-drop waterfall east of the Rocky Mountains (15 minutes by car from Ithaca).

 Delve into the history and voluptuous beauty of glass at the Corning Museum of Glass (50 minutes by car from Ithaca).

Opposite from top right: Towers of wisdom inside Uris Library; Moosewood's farm-to-table dining; campus life at Cornell University

FIRST-TIME TIPS

To celebrate Ithaca's claim as the home of the ice cream sundae, drop by the Cornell Dairy Bar, run by the College of Agriculture and Life Sciences.

Central New York grows some of the world's crunchiest, sweetest and tangiest apples, including several varieties developed by Cornell agronomists.

The Johnson Museum of Art exhibits objects from civilizations both ancient and modern, in addition to staging innovative contemporary art exhibits.

For a little corner of heaven, walk down the steep, tree-shaded trail behind Cornell's Risley Hall to the banks of Fall Creek.

Lambertville New Jersey

ON THE BANKS OF THE DELAWARE, THE RIVER THAT MADE AMERICA

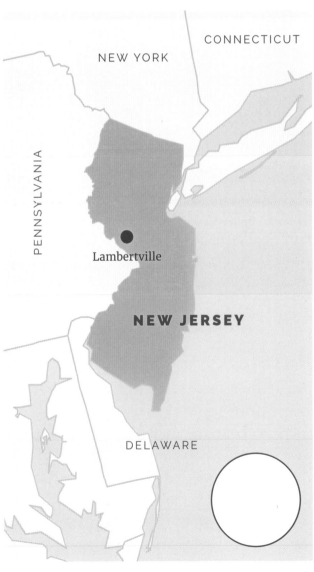

The Delaware River tells the story of the United States' birth, from George Washington's daring crossing in 1776 to the annual shad run up from the Atlantic that saved the colonists from starvation. The Lambertville Lock on the Delaware and Raritan Canal was a key to coal delivery from the Pennsylvania mines to New York City; the Belvidere–Delaware Railroad served a similar purpose.

New Jersey's bucolic Lambertville acts as a bridge to America's past, and a literal connection to Pennsylvania on the opposite shore. You may imagine, walking past 18th-century brick-fronted and colorfully painted homes, the days when Washington's troops crossed at Coryell's Ferry (Lambertville's former name) and cast nets for the fish that saved a nation.

Chummy cafes vie with white-tablecloth eateries, while custom ice-cream sandwich shops and creameries are in friendly competition with wine purveyors and distilleries, and there's plenty of walking biking, and shopping. New Jersey's Antiques Capital will keep you on your toes, eyes peeled for bargains.

GO IF YOU LIKE…
- *Revolutionary history*
- *river walks*
- *antiques*
- *art galleries*
- *fishing*
- *cycling*

Why go to Lambertville?

Ditch your car keys and stroll the quaint streets, carefree. Everything's within walking distance, from noteworthy art galleries and antique stores (you may need trunk space in the car) to sidewalk and riverfront restaurants, spanning Americana to Argentinian and French bistros to BBQ. And don't miss the Oaxaca cuisine, well-represented in restaurants like El Tule and Aztlan. Cheesemongers and chocolatiers, meanwhile, proffer mouthwatering wares side by side in storefronts.

This New Jersey burg hosts more mature bars – versus somewhat rowdier New Hope, PA – where you can duck into a few dark-paneled gin joints to ease your mind after a day of antiquing.

History buffs can tour revolutionary war sites, railroad museums and walk or bike for miles along the Raritan and Delaware Canal Towpath. In the spring, celebrate the great migration and spawning at the Annual Shad Festival honoring the town's iconic fish, and watch the last of the fishers cast off from Lewis Island.

GETTING THERE

TransBridge bus line shuttles passengers back and forth from New York's Port Authority (two hours) and also services Newark and JFK Airports. Train service from New York City takes about half an hour. Rent a kayak, canoe or bike to get up and down the river or around town.

WHEN TO GO

Sep – Nov

Fall brings the best of the region's foliage in crimson, yellow and orange, and the streets are less crowded. Halloween and its run-up get the full treatment, too.

Opposite: Antiques abound along Lambertville's shopping streets. **Above, left**: Cycling along the Delaware and Raritan Canal; **right**: strumming a tune at the annual Porchfest

FIRST-TIME TIPS

Don't miss the major <u>antique bazaars</u> on River Rd outside town on your way home. The major outfitter for kayaks and canoes is also here.

Take the time to browse and appreciate the <u>galleries on Union St</u> and around town.

<u>Sister Cities Food and Shop Tours</u> give you a lay of the land and a pleased palate – chocolate, cheese and churros, anyone?

The north end of town holds less hectic vibes; Lambertville's Pennsylvania counterpart, <u>New Hope</u>, is a short stroll across the bridge and has some fun shops and eats.

AMAZING CROWD-FREE EXPERIENCES

 Bike, jog or walk the Delaware and Raritan Canal Towpath. Seventy miles of historic passageways – once the conduit from Philly to New York – cross wooden bridges and cobblestone spillways on paths once powered by mules and steam engine. Loop trails vary from 7 to 19 miles.

 Rent a kayak or canoe if your trail trek gets to Princeton, and immerse yourself in the canal's history.

 Take classes in fly-fishing or kayaking, or enroll in bike and yoga programs.

 Get mobile on the Delaware River. Big Bear Gear on River Rd will get you situated in your floating vehicle of choice: canoe, two-person raft or tube.

 Jam with locals during October's walking music fest, with bands of different stripes performing on different front porches.

 Stroll the Institute Woods in Princeton and think big thoughts, just as Albert Einstein did a century ago on one of his favorite walks.

Opposite: Camping in the serene Green River Reservoir

The Lake Champlain Islands Vermont

AN ISLAND-HOPPING ADVENTURE THROUGH ONE OF THE NATION'S LARGEST LAKES

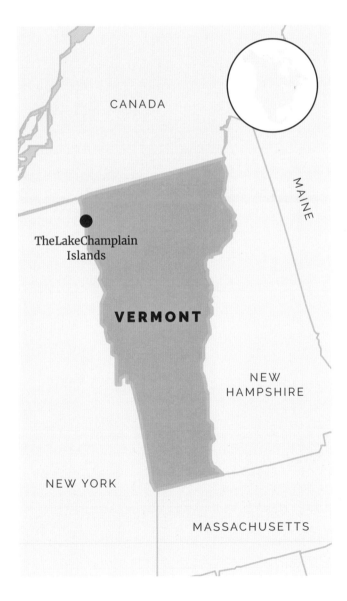

CANADA

MAINE

TheLakeChamplain
Islands

VERMONT

NEW
HAMPSHIRE

NEW YORK

MASSACHUSETTS

While Vermont is famous for its green mountains and frosty ski resorts, its islands aren't usually the subject of casual conversations. Nonetheless, the state has 71 of them on its registers, many of which are in Lake Champlain. Sprinkled throughout this 120-mile-long body of water are islands ranging from the tiny and uninhabited to those big enough to hold towns and state parks. The largest are known as the Champlain Islands located less than 30 minutes from Burlington. They include Grand Isle, North Hero, Isle La Motte and the Peninsula of Alburgh.

The Abenaki people once used these islands for hunting, fishing and agriculture. By the late 1700s, pioneers came here for farming and logging. Later, in the 20th century, the islands transitioned to tourism and became the site of summer homes and camps. Today, this offbeat getaway has bucketfuls of natural beauty, state parks, wildlife preserves and all the activities that you would expect in such a place.

GO IF YOU LIKE...
- *aquatic adventures*
- *biking*
- *sandy beaches*
- *scenic beauty*
- *state parks*
- *locally sourced cuisine*

Why go to the Lake Champlain Islands?

Home to around seven thousand people, the Champlain Islands are strung with small-town charm, boundless recreational opportunities and intriguing historical sites, allowing visitors to experience the lake without the crowds. Eight state parks make this a fantastic destination for year-round or seasonal outdoor enjoyment. In addition to camping, the parks are a great place to swim, picnic, bird-watch, hike and fish.

Step back in time with a visit to Hero's Welcome General Store in North Hero. This Vermont country store has been around for over one hundred years and carries unique local products; grab lunch from their deli counter and enjoy it on picnic tables overlooking the lake. History buffs will enjoy a visit to the Hyde Log Cabin on Grand Isle. Constructed in 1783 and inhabited by the Hyde family for over 150 years, it is thought to be among the oldest log cabins in the United States.

GETTING THERE

The Lake Champlain Islands are a pleasant 30-minute drive from downtown Burlington. From Plattsburgh on the New York side, take Lake Champlain Ferries, which runs year-round passenger, bike and car ferry services to Grand Isle. Alternatively, walkers and cyclists can take the Island Line Trail, which connects Colchester in mainland Vermont with Grand Isle.

WHEN TO GO

Jun – Oct

Temps are perfect from June to August for pretty much everything, from boating to camping. Visit after the summer peak season for fall foliage and a quieter atmosphere when the apples are ripe.

FIRST-TIME TIPS

Biking is an outstanding way to explore the mostly flat islands. There are dozens of cycling loops to explore on your own; alternatively, book a guided tour.

....

For an extended island stay, book a room at the North Hero House. This historic establishment has warmly welcomed guests since 1891, back when travelers arrived via paddle-wheel steamers.

....

Pick your own apples at Allenholm Farm, the oldest commercial apple orchard in Vermont, which has been in the Allen family since 1870.

....

Explore Isle La Motte's Fisk Quarry Preserve and Goodsell Ridge Preserve to embark on a self-guided fossil hunt.

Right: Sailboat cruising past Grand Isle's forested shore. **Opposite:** Swallows build their homes inside colorful birdboxes

© LARRY GERBRANDT / GETTY IMAGES. © LAURA KNAPP / SHUTTERSTOCK

AMAZING CROWD-FREE EXPERIENCES

 Book a campsite on Burton Island, a 253-acre park only accessible by boat. Hop aboard the state's passenger ferry to make the 10-minute trip from Kill Kare State Park.

 Grab a local beer at Two Heroes Brewery, a new brewpub in South Hero centered around community and excellent beer. This local gathering place serves pub fare alongside IPAs, lagers, ales and stouts.

 Embark on a coastal adventure to Alburgh Dunes State Park, where you'll find a natural sand beach, one of Lake Champlain's longest.

 Listen to live music at Snow Farm Vineyard every Thursday night in the summer, accompanied by wine and local beer.

 Discover one of the world's oldest coral reefs. Chazy Reef formed around 480 million years ago when Lake Champlain was a tropical sea.

 Explore the Bird House Forest at White's Beach in South Hero. Colorful birdhouses built specifically for local swallows are tacked up on nearly every tree.

North Adams Massachusetts

AN ARTSY POSTINDUSTRIAL CITY IN THE HEART OF THE BERKSHIRES

NEW HAMPSHIRE

VERMONT

North Adams

MASSACHUSETTS

NEW YORK

RHODE ISLAND

CONNECTICUT

F or over a century, artists, writers and wealthy city dwellers have retreated to the Berkshire Mountains in western Massachusetts. they built seasonal homes in picturesque villages, attending summer symphonies and theater festivals.

North Adams, meanwhile, surrounded by the same forest-covered hills and flower-filled pastures, is a 20-minute drive from the state's highest peak, Mount Greylock. But this former mill town and rundown industrial city held little appeal for vacationers.

That all started to change in 1999, when a defunct electric company was converted into the country's largest contemporary art museum, known as MassMoCA. Since then, North Adams has undergone transformation into a regional art center, with a proliferation of art galleries and an impressive assemblage of public art, not to mention popular music festivals and sophisticated dining and lodging. Now a contemporary cultural hub, North Adams is an edgy alternative (and contrast) to the region's more idyllic destinations.

GO IF YOU LIKE...
- ♥ *Asheville*
- ♥ *Durango*
- ♥ *Great Barrington*
- ♥ *contemporary art*
- ♥ *mountain hikes*
- ♥ *fall foliage*

Why go to North Adams?

MassMoCA is the creative giant in North Adams, filling its enormous exhibition halls and more than a few outdoor spaces with expectation-defying art and music. But the rest of the city is also embracing its new artistic identity. A former cotton mill now hosts live performances and a weekly art market, while another contains artist lofts and studios. A burgeoning dining scene shows off the creativity of local chefs and the bounty of regional farms. An old roadside motel has been converted into a stunning design hotel.

And an extraordinary and intriguing new attraction is in the works: the so-called Extreme Model Train and Contemporary Architecture Museum, brainchild of celebrity architect Frank Gehry.

North Adams does not offer your typical Berkshires experience: think factories instead of farmhouses, electronic instead of philharmonic. And yet…it's the same gorgeous green hills that are inspiring artists and innovators and enticing travelers. That remains blissfully unchanged.

GETTING THERE

Drive to North Adams from Boston or New York City in three to 3½ hours. Alternatively, Amtrak's *Lakeshore Limited* runs daily from Boston to nearby Pittsfield (MA) while the *Berkshire Flyer* makes the run to/from New York City on summer weekends (both about four hours). The closest airport is in Albany (NY), which is about one hour west of North Adams.

WHEN TO GO

May – Oct

The summer months are prime time for outdoor activities, cultural events and farm harvests. Solid Sound Music Festival takes place over Memorial Day weekend (the last weekend in May), while October is peak season for fall foliage.

AMAZING CROWD-FREE EXPERIENCES

 Explore the vast halls of MassMoCA. Don't miss Sol LeWitt's massive wall drawings, James Turrell's intriguing light displays and Gunnar Schonbeck's irresistible musical instruments.

 Marvel at the stunning white marble bridge over Hudson Brook, as well as the marble quarry and white marble dam at Natural Bridge State Park.

 Shop for locally made handicrafts and foodstuffs at the mini maker market at Greylock Works, a former cotton-spinning mill turned artisanal food and art hub.

 Cast your line into the Hoosic River in hopes of landing brown and rainbow trout, or take a scenic tour with Berkshire River Drifters.

 Sample the region's farm-to-table cuisine at innovative restaurants like Trailside Kitchen on the Mohawk Trail or the Breakroom at Greylock Works.

 Experience the perfect confluence of minimalist design, pristine nature and ultimate relaxation at Tourists, a refurbished motor lodge on the Mohawk Trail.

Opposite, top: The tree-lined roads to North Adams are most picturesque in fall, **bottom**: Main Street in North Adams

FIRST-TIME TIPS

Purchasing tickets in advance for [MassMoCA](#) is recommended but not required. Some specific exhibits (James Turrell, Laurie Anderson) do require advance reservations, although there is no additional charge.

....

Check out MassMoCA's jam-packed [calendar of events](#), which features live music, theater, film and dance performances, including several three-day music festivals.

....

For a self-guided tour of public art in North Adams and environs, download the [Northern Berkshire Art Outside interactive map](#) (available from the MassMoCA website).

....

Lodgings in North Adams are limited, but there are plenty more options in [Williamstown](#), five miles west.

Beyond Newport & Providence Rhode Island

WHERE SMALL TOWNS CAPTURE THE TRUE SOUL OF RHODE ISLAND

NEW HMAPSHIRE

MASSACHUSETTS

RHODE ISLAND

CONNECTICUT

Bristol, Jamestown, Tiverton, Little Compton, Westerly, Block Island, Warren, Narragansett and more.

In these smaller towns, you can experience the charming Rhode Island that residents love. There are beaches, of course – 384 miles of coastline, to be exact – but there are also sprawling vineyards, gorgeous rolling hills (yes, RI is surprisingly rural!), local art galleries, antique shops and more. There aren't many name-brand hotels in these parts (most are in Newport and Providence), but that's the point. Go for a cute Airbnb or a lovely boutique instead.

GO IF YOU LIKE...
- 🤍 *the Hamptons*
- 🤍 *Martha's Vineyard*
- 🤍 *Tuscany*
- 🤍 *fresh seafood*
- 🤍 *quaint small towns*
- 🤍 *antique shops*

When you think of Rhode Island, you probably think of the epic mansions that line the Cliff Walk in Newport, or the artsy scene in its capital Providence. And why wouldn't you? Those are the iconic Ocean State spots that show up in magazines and on TV again and again. But local Rhode Islanders and those who've been visiting for years know that the true heart and soul of 'Little Rhody' lies in the quaint, lesser-known towns sprinkled throughout the coastal state:

291

Why go beyond Newport and Providence?

Even though Rhode Island is only a 3½-hour drive from New York City and the rest of the tristate area, it hasn't gotten nearly the same attention as other popular NYC getaways like the Hamptons, the Berkshires and Nantucket. But the smaller towns in Rhode Island are the perfect escape for travelers looking for quintessential New England charm without the crowds.

And better yet, while Newport and Providence continue to grow, especially when it comes to the luxury hotel scene, these towns are way less developed and show no real signs of gentrification – meaning you can get a much more authentic, local experience when you visit. Whether you're grabbing hot dogs at the legendary Rod's Grille in Warren, the state's quirkiest town, or escaping to Block Island, the low-key answer to Nantucket and Martha's Vineyard, you will no doubt get a feel for the incredibly underrated soul of the Ocean State.

GETTING THERE

If you're flying, Rhode Island's TF Green International Airport is the most convenient, though Logan International Airport in Boston works, too. If you're coming by train or bus, alight in Providence and then rent a car to get around. If you're driving, take I-95 north or south. You can also take a one-hour high-speed ferry to Block Island from New London, Connecticut.

WHEN TO GO

May – Sep

While all New England seasons have different perks, Rhode Island truly shines in the summer – especially if you want to take advantage of its beautiful beaches and quintessential seafood joints. For classic fall foliage, trees usually peak in October.

FIRST-TIME TIPS

At the gorgeous Goosewing Beach in Little Compton, parking is free after 4pm from Memorial Day to Labor Day. Otherwise, it's $20 on weekdays and $25 on weekends.

....

For a remote experience, take the 30-minute ferry from Bristol to Prudence Island, a beautiful undeveloped island with just over one hundred year-round residents. But bring a packed lunch; there isn't a single restaurant.

....

Beavertail State Park in Jamestown is one of the best spots to watch the sunset; the rocks on the park's west side are especially photogenic. Be sure to check out the active lighthouse while you're there.

AMAZING CROWD-FREE EXPERIENCES

 Explore Colt State Park, a park right on Narragansett Bay in Bristol. Come for the hiking trails, bike paths and 4 miles of paved pathways.

 Grab a breakfast at Groundswell Cafe + Bakery, then stroll around Tiverton Four Corners.

 Enjoy a wine tasting at Carolyn's Sakonnet Vineyard in Little Compton, then relax on the grassy front lawn.

 Stop in at Evelyn's Drive-In in Tiverton for roadside fried clam strips with a side of scenic coastline.

 Hit up the beach at Watch Hill in Westerly, followed by ice cream at the legendary St Clair Annex, open since 1887.

 Take the ferry to Block Island for a fun day trip. Be sure to check out New Shoreham, the island's main town filled with shops and restaurants, and the beautiful sand dunes.

Clockwise from top left: Freshly shucked oysters; walking trails through sand dunes; the historic Ocean House Hotel

St George Maine

SEAL SPOTTING AND SUSTAINABLE SEAFOOD ON A CHARMING PENINSULA

CANADA

CANADA

MAINE

St George

VERMONT

NEW
HAMPSHIRE

This collection of quaint lobstering and fishing communities is surrounded by more than two hundred islands and located on the former hunting grounds of the Indigenous Abenaki, who formed seasonal coastal villages of fewer than one hundred residents. That tight-knit feel persists in St George (population 2594) and neighboring South Thomaston (1511) and Owls Head (1504), even after waves of American development – spanning farming, granite quarrying, shipbuilding and canning – that started in the late 1700s. Maine's charms first attracted tourists – 'rusticators' seeking summer cottages – in the 1880s.

GO IF YOU LIKE...
- ♥ *Bar Harbor*
- ♥ *Montauk*
- ♥ *lighthouses*
- ♥ *sea kayaking*
- ♥ *bird watching*
- ♥ *sunrises and sunsets*

E ven with its breathtaking shorelines, hidden trails and fresh lobster, this Midcoast Maine peninsula bookended by two lighthouses – Marshall Point and Owls Head – flies under the radar on Penobscot Bay, less than 20 miles south of the more widely traversed Camden and Rockland.

Don't come here looking for densely packed main streets. Instead you'll find a handful of beloved local art galleries, shops, accommodations and sustainable dining options and unmatched access to nature preserves and beaches.

295

Why go to St George?

Though it hasn't garnered the same level of attention as more popular alternatives, you'd be hard pressed to find a better place to experience the best of Midcoast Maine. Especially if you want to avoid crowds as you indulge in the local experiences: sustainable seafood from Port Clyde Fresh Catch, views of harbor seals and puffins from a Monhegan Boat Line cruise, Maine's best burger at Owls Head General Store and the waterfront views from one of the area's independently owned and operated B&Bs.

If you're searching for a place to slow down, unplug and reconnect with nature, the opportunities are endless, spanning from Ash Point Preserve's 1.3-mile hiking and birding trail among 34 acres of coastal spruce forest all the way to Birch Point State Park's half-moon shoreline, where the gentle waves make for invigorating swimming surrounded by evergreen trees and views of Penobscot Bay.

GETTING THERE

Travel to nearby Augusta via Greyhound or car (one hour), or to Rockland via Concord Coach Lines or car (15 minutes). Amtrak provides train service to Portland, with bus connections to Augusta. The nearest airports are in Augusta and Owls Head (13 minutes by car). I-95 and 295 connect Augusta with Boston (2½ hours).

WHEN TO GO

May – Oct

While the winters are long, cold and dark in Maine, things start to warm up by May. June through September has average temperatures in the 60s and 70s during the day, dropping into the 50s at night. Visit in mid-October for peak foliage.

FIRST-TIME TIPS

Book your accommodations in advance as the area has a <u>limited inventory of hotel rooms</u>, short-term vacation rentals, and campsites.

....

The easiest way to get around is by car, though rideshare services and <u>bike rentals</u> are available.

....

Keep in mind that cell phone coverage and Internet speeds tend to be <u>less reliable</u> in rural Maine.

....

Check the <u>opening hours</u> of local businesses as places are often closed on select weekdays and as early as 7pm.

....

Be sure to pack <u>insect repellent</u> and extra layers for cooler temperatures at night. Do nightly tick checks.

Opposite, left: Coils of rope at Port Clyde Harbor; right: fishing boats ply the waters around Monhegan Island. Above: A swimming hole in Clark Island Preserve

AMAZING CROWD-FREE EXPERIENCES

 Appreciate the area's best coastline views at the Marshall Point Lighthouse at the southernmost tip of the St George peninsula and the Owls Head State Park and Lighthouse at the northeast tip of the Owls Head peninsula.

 Sip a sustainably brewed beer made from locally grown grain at the family-owned Waterman's Beach Brewery.

 Paddle among porpoises, shore birds, lobstermen and private islands on a guided tour with Port Clyde Kayaks.

 Satisfy your cravings for Maine lobster and whoopie pie at McLoons Lobster Shack, located on a working lobster wharf on Spruce Head Island.

 Go completely car free on Monhegan Island, a protected nature reserve home to fewer than 65 year-round residents, a lobster fishing village and an artist colony.

 Get a complete nature retreat on the pedestrian-only Clark Island, a 124-acre preserve featuring a 1.8-mile loop hiking trail, secluded sandy beaches and a granite quarry turned swimming hole.

This spread:
Sayil, Yucatán, Mexico

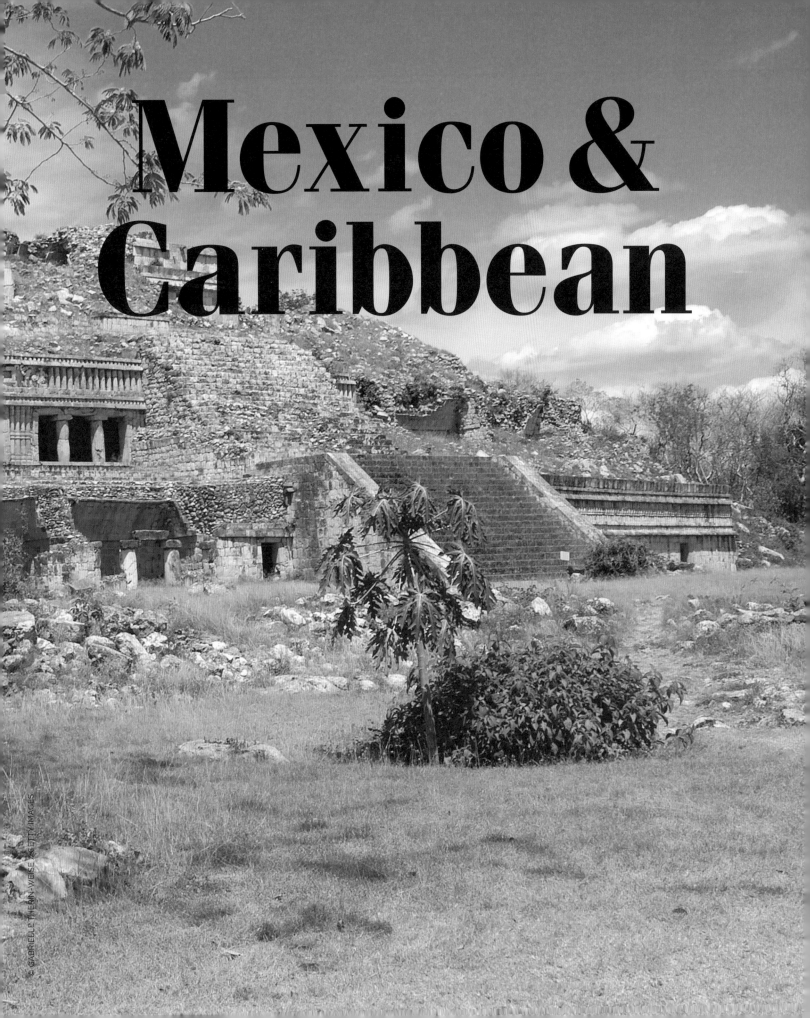

Mexico & Caribbean

Opposite: San Juan Parangaricutiro Church still stands after a volcano destroyed the surrounding village

Michoacán Mexico

CRAFTS AND NATURAL BEAUTY DEFINE AN UNDERAPPRECIATED MEXICAN STATE

TEXAS

MEXICO

Michoacán

If the crowds in Mexico City and Oaxaca leave you feeling overwhelmed, consider Michoacán, a captivating state filled with fascinating traditions and serene natural beauty. Home to the proud Purépecha people, who maintain their language, culture and artesanía (crafts), the state possesses some of the most unforgettable experiences in the country.

In Michoacán, visitors can witness hundreds of thousands of monarch butterflies flutter wing-to-wing at hilltop reserves after migrating

2500 miles south from as far as Canada. You can climb the newest volcano in the Americas, shop in towns filled with Indigenous artisans who have honed their crafts over decades, meander the marvelous Unesco-recognized pink-stone state capital Morelia and experience some of the most magical Día de Muertos celebrations in Mexico.

Unfortunately, Michoacán has a reputation for cartel-fueled violence. Government agencies in the US, the UK and Canada all advise against non-essential travel to the state, outside of Morelia. If visiting, stay away from high-conflict zones and don't travel after dark.

GO IF YOU LIKE…
- *Disney's Coco*
- *Oaxaca*
- *Day of the Dead*
- *monarch butterflies*
- *architecture*
- *climbing volcanoes*

Why go to Michoacán?

When Spanish bishop Vasco de Quiroga arrived in Michoacán in the 16th century, he proposed that local Purépecha gather in *pueblos hospitales* ('hospital towns,' but here meaning artisanal specialization), which are still active today. Support these artisans by shopping for crafts such as copperwork in Santa Clara de Cobre, feather-tipped shawls in Ahuiran and guitars in Paracho, as seen in the movie *Coco*, whose setting was partly based on Michoacán. Or hire a local guide and spend a night or two in Angahuan, from where you can climb the still-steaming Volcán Paricutín, which last erupted from 1943 to 1952. Visitor dollars help residents of the former towns destroyed by the volcano. And while the 2500-mile monarch-butterfly migration from Canada to Michoacán has been occurring for 10,000 years, it's increasingly at risk due to climate change and illegal deforestation. More travelers can steer locals to tourism jobs instead.

GETTING THERE

Morelia has an international airport and is well-connected with major Mexican cities by bus. Once in Morelia, you can easily take a bus or shared taxi to Pátzcuaro or Uruapan. Shared minibuses or taxis can take you to small towns, or you can hire a local Purépecha guide for a more in-depth experience.

WHEN TO GO

Oct – Dec

Fall marks Michoacán's dry season, the Day of the Dead celebration and the monarch butterfly migration (locals believe butterflies are souls returning home).

FIRST-TIME TIPS

Even though Michoacán is off the radar for many international travelers, you'll need to reserve accommodation well in advance for Day of the Dead due to its popularity among Mexicans.

Visit the Monarch Butterfly Reserve during the migration period from November to March. Be considerate, quiet and leave no trace while you're there.

Avoid traveling between cities at night. Also avoid the southern Tierra Caliente region and the cartel-controlled coast. Walking around downtown Morelia and Pátzcuaro at night is fine.

AMAZING CROWD-FREE EXPERIENCES

 Climb the newest volcano in the Americas, Volcán Paricutín, and visit the eerie ruins of the San Juan Parangaricutiro Church, which is protruding from black volcanic rock.

 Venture out to lesser-visited craft towns like San José de Gracia (painted pineapples), Patambam (pottery) and Ocumicho (painted acrylic masks and figurines).

 Taste mescal at Tata in Morelia and Mezcalería San Miguel in Pátzcuaro. Michoacán's distillers rival those in Oaxaca.

 Visit ruins that are more than one thousand years old at Tzintzuntzan and Tingambato in lieu of the busier Teotihuacan near Mexico City.

 Take a small boat to Janitzio, a tiny island in the middle of Lake Pátzcuaro, and climb up a giant monument to Mexican War of Independence hero José María Morelos.

 Explore a pretty national park in the heart of Uruapan and travel to the Tzararacua waterfall just outside the city.

Clockwise from top left: Craftsman assembling a guitar; la Catrina figurines; marigolds adorn the cemetery on Janitzio Island

Santiago Apoala Oaxaca, Mexico

DRAMATICALLY SITUATED HIGHLANDS IN THE HEART OF OAXACA'S MIXTEC REGION

under the radar? It's mainly because visitors in Oaxaca gravitate toward the culturally rich capital or the alluring southern coast, leaving little if any time for a journey up north.

If they only knew what they were missing. Sitting pretty in a fertile valley 6463 feet above sea level, Santiago Apoala stands as a shining example of what a successful community-run ecotourism venture should look like. Not only is the sustainable tourism project a boon for the local economy, but it also rewards travelers with life-affirming experiences as they connect with nature and the Indigenous villagers.

GO IF YOU LIKE...
- the Pueblos Mancomunados
- Mixtec culture
- sustainable tourism
- hiking and biking
- astonishing landscapes
- digital detox

Nestled in remote mountains in northern Oaxaca's seldom-visited Mixtec country, Santiago Apoala makes for an epic escape from increasingly over-touristed Oaxaca City. Just imagine a place where mighty waterfalls plunge into turquoise swimming holes, Yosemite-like rock formations rise high above deep canyons and ancient cave paintings reveal a pre-Hispanic history that dates back well over four thousand years. So why does this Mixtec wonderland continue to fly

Why go to Santiago Apoala?

Known as the cradle of Mixtec culture, Santiago Apoala is a small and welcoming town of about one thousand inhabitants where visitors can have an up-close communion with the predominantly Indigenous locals. Upon arrival, check in at Ecoturismo Comunal Yutsa To'on, the community's tourism cooperative that oversees lodging; a nominal visitor's fee includes a guided tour along one of three hiking routes. The most popular trail leads to the impressive Cola de Serpiente (Serpent's Tail) and Cola de Caballo (Horse's Tail) waterfalls, each more than 165 feet high and graced with enticing natural pools. Along the other footpaths, guides take you to hidden caves and sublime gorges while pointing out pre-Hispanic paintings and rock carvings, including a cliffside relief of an ancient dancing figure called a *danzante*. Of course, you're free to explore the sights on your own, or simply chill in a serene riverside eatery while indulging in delectable Mixtec comfort food.

Opposite, top: Canyons and crystalline waterfalls are common in this rugged part of Mexico; **bottom**: sheep grazing in the town's outskirts

FIRST-TIME TIPS

Stay in the rustic adobe cabins by the river for glorious views of the rugged mountains and fields.

....

Bring plenty of cash (no ATMs here) and keep in mind that wi-fi in the village is spotty at best.

....

Pressed for time? Tierraventura Ecotours and Coyote Aventuras run day trips from Oaxaca City to Santiago Apoala.

....

Camping is possible, but you'll need to stock up on supplies in Nochixtlan.

....

If you have a car, the quickest and most scenic route from Nochixtlan is accessed from Calle 5 de Mayo.

AMAZING CROWD-FREE EXPERIENCES

 Cool off in an aquamarine swimming hole below roaring waterfalls, then mosey down to a series of tranquil lagoons where you'll likely have the water all to yourself.

 Marvel at imposing twin peaks along a riverside trail that cuts through a 1300-foot-deep canyon. It's a relatively easy hike to tackle on your own.

 Gaze at ancient cave paintings, rock carvings and 4000-year-old glyphs while learning about Mixtec history from local guides.

 Feast on uniquely savory *mole* dishes and down-home *memelas* (corn-based snacks) and you'll understand why Oaxaca gets props as one of Mexico's top foodie destinations.

 Climb soaring rock formations or take a long-distance bike ride with Oaxaca City–based Bicicletas Pedro Martinez for an exhilarating spin around the surrounding countryside.

 Duck into the town library to see fascinating copies of ancient Mixtec codices, then head up to a panoramic lookout for a bird's-eye view of the age-old village.

GETTING THERE

Santiago Apoala is about three hours northwest of the Oaxaca International Airport by car. Alternatively, from downtown Oaxaca City, passenger vans (Transportes Turisticos de Nochixtlan) leave every half hour from Calle Galeana to Asuncion Nochixtlan, where you can catch a taxi to Santiago Apoala. Buses departing from Oaxaca's first-class ADO station serve Nochixtlan as well.

WHEN TO GO

Oct & Nov

A visit at the tail end of the rainy season allows you to stand in awe before gushing waterfalls, plus the first days of November bring colorful Day of the Dead festivities throughout Oaxaca.

San Juan Chamula Chiapas, Mexico

PAGANISM MEETS CATHOLICISM IN AN UNORTHODOX MAYAN VILLAGE

MEXICO

San Juan Chamula

While Indigenous life and globalized modernism coexist here, it's the blending of pre-Hispanic Tzotzil customs with traditional Catholic practices that feels distinctly outside the realm. It's most immediately evident in local dress – men don loose wool tunics (white or black depending on the weather), and women wear plainer white or blue blouses, as well as shawls and woolen skirts. However, it's inside the village church that things begin to get really interesting. And the Chamulan's historic tendencies toward political rebellion have earned the village rare autonomous status within Mexico: its society is governed by the community's proprietary rule of law, on which the Mexican state has no say whatsoever.

D eep in the Chiapas highlands at an altitude of 7200 feet, something different this way comes. In San Juan Chamula, a fascinating, seemingly frozen-in-time village, live the radically independent and fiercely traditional Tzotzil (Maya) community. And it is here that their fusion of Catholicism and Mayan ritual has resulted in some of North America's most curious religious practices.

GO IF YOU LIKE...

- 🤍 *off-the-beaten-path villages*
- 🤍 *religious history*
- 🤍 *esoteric theology*
- 🤍 *cathedrals*
- 🤍 *Coca-Cola™*
- 🤍 *paganism*

309

Why go to San Juan Chamula?

The syncretistic beliefs and customs of the Chamulans are unlike anything else in North or Central America. A blanket of *ramas de pinocho* (a type of local pine needle) and hundreds of illuminated candles line the floor of the Templo de San Juan Bautista, the village's house of worship, which is guarded around the clock to avoid the ever-present risk of fire. Pews are strikingly absent, incense burners billow clouds of perfumed smoke and chanting curanderos (medicine men) employ eggs and bones as curative measures. Devotees guzzle Coca-Cola and other sodas to burp out evil spirits. Chickens are sacrificed. To put things mildly, this ain't your grandmother's Sunday school. San Juan Chamula is one of the last bastions of Mayan ritual and, as such, it is a place to be respected and celebrated. Visitors are welcomed so long as they follow the rules.

GETTING THERE

The closest airport to San Juan Chamula is Tuxtla Gutiérrez's Ángel Albino Corzo International Airport (TGZ), 85km southwest of town. The village has direct connections with San Cristóbal de Las Casas, 10km to the southeast. Coletivos (shared taxis) from San Cristóbal's market and taxis make the short trip to town.

WHEN TO GO

Mar – May

San Juan Chamula enjoys a temperate climate with year-round highs that range from the mid-60s to mid-70s, with March to May being the warmest. Carnaval, held five days before Ash Wednesday, is the most festive time in town.

FIRST-TIME TIPS

It is _strictly forbidden to take photos_ or videos inside the church – doing so risks a broken camera, assault or arrest. Do not photograph locals without asking permission.

Consider visiting on an organized tour; _local guidance is invaluable_. Get Your Guide (getyourguide. com) runs trips.

San Juan Chamula is governed by local rules – neither the Mexican police nor the army will enter town – so _be respectful_ and, above all else, be on your best behavior.

Avoid visiting on Wednesday, when local superstitions leave the church empty.

AMAZING CROWD-FREE EXPERIENCES

 Observe mesmerizing rituals inside Templo San Juan Bautista. The small fee charged to enter San Juan Chamula's church buys a ticket to an otherworldly realm.

 Stroll San Juan Chamula's Sunday market. The sights, sounds and smells of the local market are a functioning exercise in village capitalism.

 Wander the village cemetery and ruins. The ruins of the 17th-century Church of San Sebastian, destroyed by fire, is surrounded by graves adorned with crosses.

 Visit a weaving cooperative in nearby Zinacantán. The Tzotzil village is prized for textiles made using the traditional backstrap loom technique.

 Indulge in local specialties. Look out for *pox* (pronounced 'posh'), a regional brandy made from fermented corn, and sweets made from *chilacayote* (fig-leaf squash).

 Cleanse your soul with shaman Juanito, who stands at the entrance of the main church. It's one of the few rituals in which outsiders can participate.

Clockwise from top left: Scarves embroidered by indigenous Tzotzil women; handweaving requires a delicate touch; headstones at an old Mayan cemetery

Ruta Puuc Yucatan, Mexico

MAGNIFICENT MAYA ARCHITECTURE ON A LESS-EXPLORED YUCATÁN ROUTE

Over 2.5 million visitors flock to Chichén Itzá every year, while popular Uxmal receives around 400,000. But few people make it to Labná, Sayil and Xlapak, the three peaceful sites of the Ruta Puuc proper, which have been part of the wider Uxmal Unesco World Heritage Site since the 1990s. Labná and Sayil are believed to have once had thousands of inhabitants; tiny Xlapak, meanwhile, is thought to have been an agricultural hub for the Puuc region. Their richly adorned buildings and distinctive Puuc style mark a high point in Maya architecture. Even in the peak season, these monuments receive only around 3500 monthly visitors combined.

While Mexico's deservedly famous Maya headliner Chichén Itzá tends to steal the show, many quieter, lesser-known Maya relics lie hidden away in the hilly Puuc region south of Yucatán's culture-rich capital Mérida. In the southernmost part of Yucatán, bordering neighboring Campeche, the Ruta Puuc weaves together a string of little-visited Maya ruins, where intricately carved palaces emerge from dense forests. It makes a magical counterpart to lively Mérida.

GO IF YOU LIKE...

🤍 *Maya architecture*
🤍 *Chichén Itzá*
🤍 *regional cuisine*
🤍 *Uxmal and Kabah*
🤍 *ancient civilizations*
🤍 *Mexican history*

Why go to Ruta Puuc?

Dotted along a forest-shaded road, 10 to 15 miles southeast of Santa Elena village, the Ruta Puuc's sites are smaller and (in some cases) less maintained than their more famous Maya siblings, but therein lies the beauty. On a cool morning, there's often no one else in sight.

This fertile, undulating pocket of Yucatán is known for its especially elaborate Puuc-style buildings and detailed carvings, which typically include the Maya rain deity, Chaac. Strolling across a sun-drenched courtyard to gaze at the beautifully carved El Palacio at Labná (the most thrilling of the three complexes) or wandering down a dusty forest trail before stumbling across a half-lost building at Sayil, it's impossible not to feel the weight of this once-powerful civilization.

Labná's monumental arch is the big showstopper, but there's plenty more to discover, particularly if you allow time for exploring beyond the main buildings, as not everything has been fully excavated.

GETTING THERE

The route begins 70 miles south of Mérida (a 90-minute drive), where a smaller road branches off Hwy 261 toward Sayil then continues on to Xlapak and Labná. It's best to explore with your own wheels. Arrive early, make the most of the drive and enjoy the monuments at your preferred pace. There are also guided tours from Mérida with local operators.

WHEN TO GO

Sep – Apr

Skip the hot, humid summer months, which are usually busy across the Yucatán Peninsula. The weather cools down from September onward, and the crowds thin out, too.

AMAZING CROWD-FREE EXPERIENCES

 At Labná, wander beneath the soaring 10-foot-wide corbelled arch decorated with Puuc reliefs. Explore the impressive raised El Palacio and gaze at the crumbling temple-topped pyramid El Mirador; the site is believed to have peaked from 600 CE to 1000 CE.

 For a taste of rural Yucatán, base yourself in the pastel-painted village of Santa Elena overnight instead of day-tripping from Mérida. The Pickled Onion has palapa-roof rooms and Yucatecan food (thepickledonionyucatan.com).

 Enjoy the meandering drive between the Maya monuments – it's all part of the Ruta Puuc experience.

 The region's sparkling cenotes are perfect for cooling off; ask locally about what's open.

 Admire Sayil's three-tiered El Palacio complex; ornately carved masks of Chaac and Puuc columns are among the architectural highlights of a city that thrived between 800 CE and 1000 CE, reaching a population of 10,000.

 Explore small Xlapak, where an intricate palace features Puuc pillars, Chaac masks and ornamental latticework.

Opposite, left: The Gateway Arch at Labna; **right**: Chaac (rain deity) masks at Palace I in Xlapak. **Above**: A motorized cart on the streets of Santa Elena

Samaná Dominican Republic

**BREACHING WHALES, QUIET BEACHES AND
A COZY TOWN FAR FROM RESORT-SATURATED HUBS**

CUBA

HATI

JAMAICA

Santiago
Apoala

**DOMINICAN
REPUBLIC**

CARIBBEAN SEA

Dominican charm. Sure, it takes an extra 30 minutes from Santo Domingo's airport to get there, and yes, portions of the drive can be super windy. But for those wanting to truly explore – be it kayaking through mangroves and navigating the petroglyph-marked caves at Haitises National Park or cracking open an ice-cold Presidente beer with a local at a comedor (family-owned restaurant or bar) in town – this is turquoise water–surrounded bliss.

GO IF YOU LIKE...
- *whale watching*
- *island adventure*
- *quiet coastlines*
- *boating journeys*
- *fresh-caught seafood*
- *rainforest hikes*

Punta Cana gets the bulk of the Dominican Republic's tourist love. Dotted with white sand expanses and mega all-inclusive resorts, the city at the country's easternmost tip is home to approximately 50% of the country's hotel rooms. At the opposite end of the 'stay put at the resort' and 'don't venture too far from your hotel's gates' spectrum is the Samaná Peninsula. Compared to its Punta Cana counterpart, this is a place that's ripe for an adventure: it has tropical wildlife, less-congested beaches, an expansive mountains-meets-sea bay landscape and the most authentic

Why go to Samaná?

The region's most prized beaches remain visibly unscathed, be it Rincón Beach with mangrove swamps and shack-style bars or the 1.8-mile-long Bonita Beach with its towering coconut trees and golden sands. When you need a reprieve from the beach life, the Museo de las Ballenas (Whale Museum) zooms in on the history of the local humpback population, with a giant skeleton connecting its two principal rooms.

While Samaná's shores aren't cluttered with soaring resorts, it is starting to slowly welcome more sustainable accommodations. Among them, Cayo Levantado Resort opened in June 2023 on a boat-accessible Bacardi Island, known for being the site of the brand's first commercial shoots in the 1980s. A wellness lover's dream, it's anchored by a palapa-covered 'Yubarta' in the island's center – with sound healing, cenotes, breathing workshops and more. Another sustainable-lodging option is Samana Ecolodge, with bungalows and treehouse rooms tucked in a jungle.

GETTING THERE

From Las Américas International Airport in Santo Domingo, downtown Samaná is a 2½-hour drive north, primarily via the country's well-paved interstates 7 and 5. In addition to rental car outposts at the airport, a number of tour operators offer shared or private shuttles to town.

WHEN TO GO

Jan – Apr

In winter, the climate is less sticky – by 10°F or so – than in the summer months, and hurricane season (Jun through Nov) is not a concern. Whale-watching season is also in its prime (Nov through Apr).

FIRST-TIME TIPS

A little Spanish can go a long way. Compared to more tourist-centric destinations in the Dominican Republic, count on needing either basic Spanish and/or a translation app.

Come boat ready. Pack motion-sickness aids, sunscreen and other ocean necessities as it's a common mode of transport for outings.

Book an ecofriendly tour. Samaná now has its own locally operated ecotourism association, Go Samaná (gosamana-dominicanrepublic.com), that provides a regularly updated list of trusted operators.

The colonial town of Santa Barbara de Samaná is known simply as 'Samaná.'

Opposite: A humpback whale somersaults in the waves. **Above**: Mangrove forests are a nursing ground for numerous fish species

AMAZING CROWD-FREE EXPERIENCES

 Trek to the Salto del Limón waterfall. Access this mossy-rock cascade and swimming hole via a 30-minute hike or horseback ride from the town of Rancho Español.

 Dine on the catch of the day. Restaurant-Bar Moreno Y Ruth is tucked on the public beach portion of Cayo Levantado, offering just-caught catches fried, grilled or doused in coconut.

 Duck through the caves of Haitises National Park. Opt for the cross-bay boat venture to explore ancient Taino petroglyphs in the caves.

 Snorkel and kitesurf at El Portillo Beach. Year-round warm waters at this beach town on the peninsula's north coast make for prime and tranquil water outings.

 Stroll through Samaná town; it has a corrugated iron church (La Chorcha), a footbridge jutting out to a nearby island and a bayside boardwalk.

 Embark on a whale-watching tour. Canada native Kim Beddall is considered the founder of commercial whale-watching in Samaná and has been giving tours since 1983.

And there's more...

25 OTHER OFFBEAT DESTINATIONS TO PUT ON YOUR RADAR

Cold Lake, Alberta

The Lakeland region of Alberta, Canada, is dotted with dozens of deep, clear bodies of water, but its star attraction is Cold Lake. Yes, the water's cold, but it's also crystal clear. Big enough to feature its own island, Cold Lake has wide sandy beaches (including some with purple sand; the result of garnet gemstones) excellent fishing, and endless opportunities for hiking, wakeboarding and paddling. Keep your eyes peeled for the Kinosoo, a mythical trout so large it could swallow a canoe.

Stehekin, WA

Framed by glorious views of the North Cascades and Lake Chelan, this remote town of approximately 90 residents is a breathtakingly beautiful oasis. No roads lead to Stehekin: a few hardy souls hike and some come by air, but most visitors arrive by boat. Make the most of a day trip by taking the Lady Express and rent bikes to ride up to Rainbow Falls. Hike the Mist Trail, head to Buckner Orchard and finish up at Stehekin Pastry Company.

Clear Lake, CA

Take Napa Valley, subtract the high prices, add Lake Tahoe, subtract the tourists, turn back the clock a few decades, and voila! You get Clear Lake. This off-the-radar wine country is little more than an hour's drive north of wildly popular Napa and Sonoma, but it's low-key and budget-friendly. A dormant, hike-worthy volcano lords above it all, and around the lake you'll find quaint lodgings and tasty restaurants. From the drive-in movie theater to the lunch-box museum, this place is a hoot.

Idyllwild, CA

Escape the heat of lowland SoCal by driving up Rte 243, and you'll start to notice the butterscotch scent of Jeffrey pines. Nestled amid forest in Mount San Jacinto State Park, 'Idyllwild' comprises Idyllwild, Pine Cove and Fern Valley. Whether you want to curl up by a fire with a book, hike miles of forested trails or do yoga followed by a glass of wine or three, you've come to the right place.

Paonia, CO

Overshadowed by bigger and better-known wine regions, like Colorado's Grand Valley and California's Napa and Sonoma, Paonia is home to some of the highest vineyards in North America. This town of just 1400 residents has 12 mom-and-pop wineries – many with sunny patios that offer sweeping views of the surrounding West Elks mountain range. Though wine is the big draw, you'll also find plenty of uncrowded outdoor adventures like hiking, mountain biking, cherry picking and camping.

The Four Corners, CO

This dramatic landscape of towering mesas and buttes, red rock canyons and high desert beauty was inhabited by the Ancestral Puebloans who left behind thousands of elaborate cliff dwellings and structures. Beyond the region's main draw, Mesa Verde National Park, are little-visited national monuments like Hovenweep and Canyons of the Ancients. Explore a treasure trove of trails through stunning canyons to ancient villages, their sacred kivas and towers still intact, or follow a Ute guide onto Ute Mountain Tribal Park, clambering up ladders to magnificent cliff dwellings.

Tahlequah, OK

Nestled in the foothills of the Ozarks, this small town is where many Cherokee people settled after their forced removal from ancestral lands in the Southeast. In 1839, Tahlequah became the capital of both the Cherokee Nation and the United Keetoowah Band of Cherokee Indians. Today, it preserves and celebrates Cherokee heritage through well-funded museums, historic sights and tribal events. Independent travelers are few but those who visit are given a unique opportunity to meet people from the USA's largest tribe, hear the Otali dialect spoken and eat traditional foods.

Cahokia Mounds, IL

Once upon a time, one of the world's greatest cities — Cahokia — rose like the sun on the horizon of the Midwestern prairie. Built by the native Mississippians, this sophisticated, prosperous capital was larger than London, its population reaching circa 20,000 between 1050 and 1150. Today, the remnants of Cahokia, the most sophisticated prehistoric native civilization north of Mexico, are carefully preserved at Cahokia Mounds State Historic Site, located just a few miles off Route 66, west of Collinsville, Illinois.

Red Cliffs National Conservation Area, UT

Las Vegas getaways usually focus on the Grand Canyon, Death Valley and Zion. But to escape busloads of day-trippers, consider Red Cliffs instead. A unique ecological transition zone, where the Colorado Plateau, the Great Basin and the Mojave Desert meet, this awe-inspiring red-rock landscape is ideal for hiking, mountain biking, horseback riding and camping, and it's a critical habitat for the Mojave Desert tortoise. Red Cliffs protects traces of human and natural history as well: it's the site of 190-million-year-old fossilized dinosaur footprints and 1500-year-old Ancestral Puebloan structures.

Pendleton, OR

While cowboy vibes prevail, especially during Rodeo Week, scratch the surface to find a place with stories to tell: from settlers braving the Oregon Trail to missionaries and outlaws. Intertwined with their stories are those of the Confederated Tribes of the Umatilla Indian Reservation, who are deeply invested in the area's present and future and run many local businesses. Explore downtown, the Blue Mountains in the southeast, and the Columbia River curving in from the northwest.

Tennessee

Other than popular Great Smoky Mountains National Park, travelers often miss good ol' Tennessee. But Tennessee has astonishing natural diversity and a whopping 56 state parks. Walk in the shade of Eastern Tennessee's oaks and poplars. Experience middle Tennessee's thundering waterfalls, and swim in the pools at Cummins Fall and Rock Island. Meanwhile western Tennessee pulls its power from the mighty Mississippi: paddle the Ghost River through bald cypress and water tupelo swamps, or bird-watch at the Hatchie Wildlife Refuge.

Above: Wheat farming in Pendleton. **Opposite**: Trails in the San Jacinto Mountains

Southwest OH

Corn fields and cows? Think again. Southwest Ohio is also where you'll find the world's only ventriloquism museum, the country's largest Oktoberfest, and the Donut Trail. The green hills and vintage architecture of Cincinnati anchor the region. Eclectic museums stash neon signs and explain the city's Underground Railroad history, while unusual festivals celebrate adult tricycle races and goetta, a pork sausage found only in Cincy. Throughout the region, an outsized food scene thrives.

St Joseph, MO

Possibly the most important historic town you've never heard of, St Jo was a major departure point for 19th-century pioneers headed for California or the Oregon Territory. The merchants who supplied these onward travelers became wonderfully wealthy, and in the mid-1800s, St Jo had the highest per-capita income of any city in the country. More than a dozen museums, historic neighborhoods of grand homes and herringbone brick sidewalks are reminders of the opulence of a bygone era.

Grand Island, NE

Many travelers overlook the Cornhusker State entirely. But this mid-sized community in central Nebraska has a living history museum, a revitalized downtown district, a burgeoning craft beer scene, multiple golf courses and a variety of antique shops and locally owned boutiques. With a colorful waterpark and fun annual events – including the beloved 'Junk Jaunt,' a statewide three-day garage sale – Grand Island welcomes families with open arms. Come in to see the millions of sandhill cranes that stop to fatten up while migrating.

Door County, WI

Door County, the Cape Cod of the Midwest. This verdant 70-mile-long peninsula has 34 named islands and dozens of charming communities. Early Scandinavian settlers left their mark on local culture; it isn't hard to find jars of lingonberries or a painted Dala horse in local shops, and fish boils are held nightly during the summer and early fall. Tip: kayaks are one of the best ways to see the limestone caves, lighthouses and rocky shoreline.

Buffalo River, AR

The USA's first national river, the glimmering Buffalo winds through the Ozarks for 135 miles, and its pristine waters and serene bends make for one of the best floats in the country. Visitors can hike and fish, but most come to this spectacular place to paddle beneath massive bedrock cliffs and across gentle riffles. Access to the Buffalo is free, and the river is also lined with well-tended campsites with easy access to the water.

Cajun Country, LA

With its Gulf Coast beaches and small-town crawfish shacks, Cajun Country stretches from the Mississippi Delta to the Texas border. The Cajuns descend from French speakers who settled in the Louisiana swamps in the 18th century, and their culture informs every aspect of life. Sample local cuisine on the Boudin Trail: a culinary journey built around Louisiana's favorite sausage, typically stuffed with pork, spices and rice. Visitors also come for bayou boat tours, fantastic fishing and the occasional glimpse of lazy gators.

Dahlonega, GA

In 1828, deer hunter Benjamin Parks stumbled over a gold-veined rock in the North Georgia Mountains, spurring America's first major gold rush. The gold is now gone, but the charming highland hamlet of Dahlonega remains, flanked vineyards. Everything radiates out from Dahlonega's lush 19th-century public square: historic buildings, cute shops, and fun bars and restaurants. The cherry on the cake: 22 Chattahoochee National Forest trails and mountain white-water and flatwater for kayaking, canoeing and tubing.

Boone, NC

When most people go hiking or brewery-hopping in North Carolina, they head to Asheville. But when people from Asheville go hiking or brewery-hopping, they head to Boone, a small town perched 3333 feet above sea level in the Blue Ridge Mountains. Boone's downtown has Southern charm by the bucketload – old-timey general store, antique stores, folk-art galleries – but there are also eclectic restaurants and microbreweries. Meanwhile, the hiking trails that wind through and around the downtown area mean that nature's never far away.

Bahia Honda State Park, FL

Stop for snorkeling, cycling and tranquil camping at this white-sand oasis, tucked away between the Florida Keys' more raucous and commercial hubs. Its shallow waters are ideal for exploring coral reefs, watching seabirds and seeing turtles nest. The Sandspur Beach was shuttered following Hurricane Irma, but reopened in 2022 with an improved 24-site campground and amenities. Rent a kayak or book an offshore boat trip; there's never been a better time to visit.

Henniker, NH

The pace is slow and steady as the Contoocook River in this historic mill town. Markers on many buildings date to the late 18th century, and a rustic feel infuses the dusty used bookshops, homemade ice cream shops and pancake cabins. Go for hiking and biking in the warmer months or winter sports.

Opposite: Downtown Cincinnati. **Below**: Dancing waters at Sandstone Falls

Erie, PA

The small town of Erie has a maritime history, flourishing arts culture and wine-making industry. Known as Gem City for the way the water sparkles, many of Erie's charms flow from the lake. Start with the historic Bayfront District, then get out on the water on Presque Isle. West of downtown, the lesser-developed Erie Bluffs State Park has lush trails leading to secluded spots on the lake.

Hartford, CT

Smack dab in the center of Connecticut, Hartford is one of America's oldest cities. Iconic American authors Mark Twain (Samuel Clemens) and Harriett Beecher Stowe made their homes in stylish West Hartford, and you can tour the houses and gardens. Bushnell Park holds the landmark capitol building and its golden dome, along with a 1914 antique merry-go-round. Meanwhile, the old and new clash spectacularly where the nine-story, glass-and-steel Connecticut Science Center juxtaposes with the Tudor-inspired castles of the Wadsworth Atheneum.

Lewes, DE

In this historic hamlet, architecture buffs can marvel at a mix of centuries-old colonial, federal and Victorian buildings. You can also go kayaking in the Delaware Bay, wandering through lavender fields at Warrington Manor and exploring Cape Henlopen State Park's green forests, wetlands and white dunes. It's one of the most bicycle-friendly states in the US, with an 11-mile pedestrian and bike trail from Lewes to Georgetown.

New River Gorge National Park, WV

America's newest national park protects a forested canyon famed for its hiking, mountain biking and rock climbing. Class IV+ white-water rafting is some of the most thrilling in the US, while BASE jumpers can legally hurl themselves over the bridge for Bridge Day. For glamping in solitude, rafting outfitters like Adventures on the Gorge and ACE Adventure Resort have riverside compounds with canvas tents, cabins and hotel-style rooms.

Index

Offbeat North America
May 2024
Published by Lonely Planet Global Limited
CRN 554153
www.lonelyplanet.com
10 9 8 7 6 5 4 3 2 1

Printed in China
ISBN 978 18375 8224 2
© Lonely Planet 2024
© photographers as indicated 2024

Publishing Director Piers Pickard
Publisher Becca Hunt
Commissioning Editor Anita Isalska
Originally designed by Daniel di Paolo
Typesetting by Lizzie Vaughan
Editors Christopher Pitts, Alison Throckmorton
Index Connie Binder
Print Production Nigel Longuet

Lonely Planet Global Limited
Digital Depot, Roe Lane (off Thomas St),
Digital Hub, Dublin 8,
D08 TCV4
Ireland

STAY IN TOUCH lonelyplanet.com/contact
Authors Alicia Underlee Nelson; Amy Balfour; Amy Bizzarri; Annie Daly; Ashley Harrell; Bailey Freeman; Brian Kluepfel; Brian Thacker; Carolyn Heller; Catherine Toth Fox; Dana Freeman; Daniel Robinson; Erin Kirkland; Greg Benchwick; Heleina Burton; Isabella Noble; Jackie Gutierrez-Jones; Jess Lockhart; Jesse Scott; Joel Balsam; John Hecht; Joshua Samuel Brown; Julekha Dash; Karla Zimmerman; Kevin Raub; Kristen Pope; Kylie Neuhaus; Lauren Keith; Liza Prado; Madison Miller; Mara Vorhees; Mary Kearl; Michele Herrmann; Regan Stephens; Sarah Gilliland; Sarah Kuta; Sarah Lempa; Sarah Sekula; Stephen Lioy; Tim Richards; Wendy Yanagihara.

Cover photograph of Bisti Badlands, New Mexico by Todd Hakala/ Getty Images
Back cover photographs by Andrew Repp/ Shutterstock, Juan Melli / Getty Images, Nagel Photography/ Shutterstock